How to Talk About Data

Pearson

At Pearson, we have a simple mission: to help people make more of their lives through learning.

We combine innovative learning technology with trusted content and educational expertise to provide engaging and effective learning experiences that serve people wherever and whenever they are learning.

From classroom to boardroom, our curriculum materials, digital learning tools and testing programmes help to educate millions of people worldwide – more than any other private enterprise.

Every day our work helps learning flourish, and wherever learning flourishes, so do people.

To learn more, please visit us at **www.pearson.com/uk**

How to Talk About Data

Build your data fluency

Martin J. Eppler
Fabienne Bünzli

 Pearson

Harlow, England • London • New York • Boston • San Francisco • Toronto • Sydney
Dubai • Singapore • Hong Kong • Tokyo • Seoul • Taipei • New Delhi
Cape Town • São Paulo • Mexico City • Madrid • Amsterdam • Munich • Paris • Milan

Pearson Education Limited
KAO Two
KAO Park
Harlow CM17 9NA
United Kingdom
Tel: +44 (0)1279 623623
Web: www.pearson.com/uk

First edition published 2022 (print and electronic)

ISBN: 978-1-292-42119-3 (print)
       978-1-292-42121-6 (PDF)
       978-1-292-42120-9 (ePub)

British Library Cataloguing-in-Publication Data
A catalogue record for the print edition is available from the British Library

Library of Congress Cataloging-in-Publication Data
A catalog record for the print edition is available from the Library of Congress

10 9 8 7 6 5 4 3 2 1
26 25 24 23 22

Cover design by Rogue Four Design

Print edition typeset in 9.5/13, ITC Giovanni Std by Straive
Printed by Ashford Colour Press Ltd, Gosport

NOTE THAT ANY PAGE CROSS REFERENCES REFER TO THE PRINT EDITION

Contents

Overview of figures and tables

Pearson's Commitment to Diversity, Equity and Inclusion

Pearson is dedicated to creating bias-free content that reflects the diversity, depth and breadth of all learners' lived experiences. We embrace the many dimensions of diversity including, but not limited to, race, ethnicity, gender, sex, sexual orientation, socioeconomic status, ability, age and religious or political beliefs.

Education is a powerful force for equity and change in our world. It has the potential to deliver opportunities that improve lives and enable economic mobility. As we work with authors to create content for every product and service, we acknowledge our responsibility to demonstrate inclusivity and incorporate diverse scholarship so that everyone can achieve their potential through learning. As the world's leading learning company, we have a duty to help drive change and live up to our purpose to help more people create a better life for themselves and to create a better world.

Our ambition is to purposefully contribute to a world where:

- Everyone has an equitable and lifelong opportunity to succeed through learning.
- Our educational products and services are inclusive and represent the rich diversity of learners.
- Our educational content accurately reflects the histories and lived experiences of the learners we serve.
- Our educational content prompts deeper discussions with students and motivates them to expand their own learning and worldview.

We are also committed to providing products that are fully accessible to all learners. As per Pearson's guidelines for accessible educational Web media, we test and retest the capabilities of our products against the highest standards for every release, following the WCAG guidelines in developing new products for copyright year 2022 and beyond. You can learn more about Pearson's commitment to accessibility at:

https://www.pearson.com/us/accessibility.html

While we work hard to present unbiased, fully accessible content, we want to hear from you about any concerns or needs regarding this Pearson product so that we can investigate and address them.

- Please contact us with concerns about any potential bias at:

  https://www.pearson.com/report-bias.html

- For accessibility-related issues, such as using assistive technology with Pearson products, alternative text requests, or accessibility documentation, email the Pearson Disability Support team at:

  disability.support@pearson.com

About the authors

Martin J. Eppler, PhD, vice rector of the University of St Gallen, holds the chair of communications management at the School of Management and he is a director of the institute for media and communications management. His research interests include data communication, visualisation as well as analytics biases. He is the author of 23 books and more than 300 academic articles. He has been an advisor and trainer to organisations such as the European Central Bank, the UN or Swiss Re.

Fabienne Bünzli, PhD, is an award-winning researcher and lecturer at the University of St Gallen. She has also been a visiting assistant professor at the Pennsylvania State University. Fabienne Bünzli studies the persuasive effects of visual communication on individuals' attitudes and behaviours using quantitative data and statistics. Her work has been published in peer-reviewed journals and has been presented at international conferences. Prior to her work in academia, Fabienne Bünzli gained extensive experience in communications as a PR specialist, media analyst and journalist.

Acknowledgements

This book is not just the result of many conversations among its two authors, but also with several guides on the side.

We would like to thank Eloise Cook from Pearson Education for the constructive dialogues about the manuscript of this book and for her many insightful suggestions. She truly is an advocate for all readers out there.

We would also like to thank Professor Christian Hildebrand of the University of St. Gallen's TechX Lab for his instructive feedback and suggestions on state-of-the-art analytics. Special thanks also to Andreas Göldi from btov Partners and to Markus Aeschimann from Medbase for giving us feedback on early chapters of this book.

A final and heartfelt thank you goes to the many talented analytics professionals and managers at various organisations with whom we had the privilege to test out the key ideas documented in this data fluency guide. We want to thank the analytics community at Swiss Re – especially Patricia Stone, Patrick Veenhoff, Stefan Sieger and Bianca Scheffler – but also those working in analytics at the European Central Bank, at Heinemann, at Interactive Things, at Frontwerks and at the International Committee of the Red Cross.

Martin J. Eppler and Fabienne Bünzli

Publisher's acknowledgements

Photo Credits:

20 **Shutterstock:** Andrey_Popov/Shutterstock; 35 **Shutterstock:** vgstudio/ Shutterstock; 35 **Shutterstock:** Andresr/Shutterstock; 35 **Shutterstock:** R. Gino Santa Maria/Shutterstock; 35 **Shutterstock:** Monkey Business Images/Shutterstock; 35 **Shutterstock:** Maridav/Shutterstock; 35 **Shutterstock:** szefei/Shutterstock; 35 **123RF:** javiindy/123RF

Text Credits:

10 **Baruch Spinoza:** Quoted by Baruch Spinoza; 10 **Ralph C. Smedley:** Quoted by Ralph C. Smedley; 26 **Simply Psychology:** Saul McLeod, What is Kurtosis? 2019. Retrieved from https://www.simplypsychology. org/kurtosis.html; 38, 57, 61, 62, 65, 73, 95 and 98 **SAGE Publications:** Field, A. (2018). Discovering statistics using IBM SPSS statistics (5th ed). Sage Publications; 49, 58 and 61 **O'Reilly Media, Inc.:** Griffiths, D. (2009). Head first statistics. A brain-friendly guide. O'Reilly UK Ltd.; 50 **Medium Corporation:** Ramanjaneyulu Thanniru, Linear Regression, 2020. Retrieved from https://medium.com/@ram420/ linear-regression-bebe2485415a; 53 **Wolters Kluwer:** Akoglu, User's guide to correlation coefficients, Turk J Emerg Med. 2018, 18(3): 91–93; 61 **Pearson Education:** Field, A. (2018). Discovering statistics using IBM SPSS statistics (5th ed.). Sage; Griffiths, D. (2009). Head first statistics. A brain-friendly guide. O'Reilly UK Ltd.; 105 Herbert Simon: Quoted by Herbert Simon; 135 **William Shakespeare:** Quoted by William Shakespeare; 147 **Peter Drucker:** Quoted by Peter Drucker; 163 **Valérie M. Saintot:** ECB Meeting Lab. Used with permissions; 166 **Matthew Arnold:** Quoted by Matthew Arnold.

Preface

Our aim with this book is to empower you to build a skill called *data fluency* and to lead high-quality analytics conversations with diverse groups of people in your organisation. We believe that our highly visual approach and our use of vivid, real-life dialogues and simple, varied examples will speed up your learning progress and make *your journey to data fluency* a more seamless – and hopefully entertaining – one. To start, ask yourself this question:

What is the most powerful tool to make sense of data?

If you're thinking about a giant relational database, a powerful machine learning algorithm, a clever Python library or a sophisticated R script, think again.

Yes, you certainly need enormous databases to harness the power of big data. And yes, algorithms that can autonomously learn from data are a key element to derive relevant patterns out of a constant stream of data. We also agree that Python and R are two of the most widely used programming approaches to 'torture data till it speaks to you'. But there is an even more powerful tool to make sense of data, as you will discover in this book.

The most powerful tool for making sense of data is a good conversation.

It is through conversations that business requirements are translated into analytics endeavours and data queries.

It is through conversations that query results and data reports are shared, scrutinised, put into a wider context and ultimately made applicable.

There cannot be high-quality data analytics without high-quality conversations. For data to become truly valuable, it must be part of our everyday discussions.

Yet in reality, such conversations often break down or derail. Data analysts and managers don't speak the same language, have radically different perspectives or lack insights into each other's methods and constraints. This at times makes reaching a common view on data difficult.

There are two keys to master this challenge and you can find both of them in this book.

First, we all need to understand the basics of data by establishing a solid comprehension of elementary statistics (and its terminology), as statistics *is* the language of data. In this effort, we need to make things as simple as possible (but not simpler, as Einstein noted) and be aware of potential biases in our data.

This will enable us to talk about data *competently* and *critically*.

Second, we need to be able to *design good data dialogues* to make analytics work in organisations. We need to know how to ask good questions about data, how to (interactively) present and visualise data, and how to tell good data stories.

This will enable us to talk about data *clearly*.

It has certainly been an interesting journey for ourselves to write this communication guide to data analytics. To make this book a reality, the two of us had numerous constructive conversations with a variety of colleagues whom we'd like to thank at this point.

Introduction: Your guide to data fluency

The highest activity a human being can attain is learning for understanding, because to understand is to be free.

Baruch Spinoza (17th century Philosopher)

Understanding comes through communication.

Ralph C. Smedley (founder of Toastmasters International)

What you'll learn

In this short introduction, we first clarify the need for this book. We then define the notion of data fluency and its key elements, and we outline the main objectives of the book, as well as its approach and overall structure. You will also learn how each chapter is organised in terms of recurring text elements.

If you are reading this, then you have already realised how crucial it is for everyone today to understand data and how it is analysed. You are aware of the ever-growing importance of data in today's world, and you know that data is a key enabler for success and progress in business, society, and even for your own wellbeing (think of medical data or your health tracking devices). You may also be aware of the risks inherent in using data incorrectly or with a narrow mindset.

This book enables you to speak competently about data with others – whether data specialists or people with a modest data literacy – to make sense of it and apply it to decisions at hand.

Having read this book, you will have acquired a skill called *data fluency*. Data fluency refers to the ability to **talk competently, clearly and critically about data** with others by having grasped the key concepts of analytics (including the statistical terms and procedures behind it) and knowing how to apply them in organisational settings.

The premise of this book is that data fluency has become an essential business skill for anyone and that this skill can be learned. A second, related premise is that deep understanding comes from good communication. Good communication can help us get the most value out of data and assess its quality better – thus ultimately enabling us to make better, more informed decisions. Communicating with data is a skill that anyone can use, whether you are a business leader, a non-profit manager, a project coordinator or a functional specialist.

More specifically, data fluency includes such skills as asking the right questions about data, telling captivating stories about data, visualising data clearly or handling data disagreements constructively. These are relevant skills for many areas of life, from developing a business to launching an NGO; from developing a strategy to devising a funding plan; from understanding your customers to managing risks. The following diagram (you will see this format in every chapter by the way) summarises these elements and gives a few examples that we will discuss in the book.

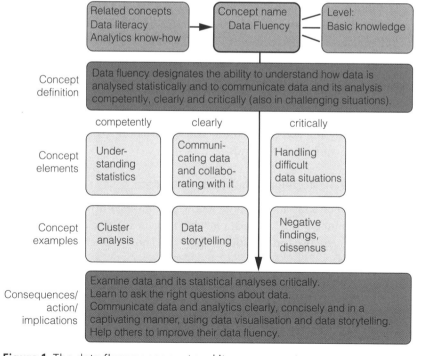

Figure 1 The data fluency concept and its components.

Data fluency allows you to understand the language of data, but also to translate this into everyday language.

What's our journey to data fluency in this book? Let us briefly take you through the different chapters and what you will learn in each one. We have structured this concise guide into two parts. Part 1 provides you with a solid basis in the statistics that you need to grasp to understand data analytics. It not only contains many examples of common data analysis misconceptions and how to avoid them, but also advice on how to make statistical procedures or terms accessible to anyone in your organisation. Part 2 of the book expands on this and focuses on how to discuss data and analytics with others.

Overview of chapters

Part 1: Understanding data

Chapter 1: How to improve your data fluency

To start our dive into the wonderful world of analytics, we offer a brief reality check on why many of us shy away from data and its statistical analysis. We show the seven drivers that lead people to be afraid of data when they really shouldn't be and how this book helps address this kind of anxiety effectively.

Chapter 2: Making sense of statistics

This chapter gives you the essentials to analyse and make sense of your data. This involves the basic concepts you need to know to talk about data confidently and accurately. You will also learn how to get an overview of your data and a feel for trends.

Chapter 3: Modelling the world with data

This chapter aims at equipping you with the capability to identify patterns in your data and understand what they mean. We clarify how to use data for predictive (prognostic) purposes and how to infer generalisations from data.

Chapter 4: Understanding complex relationships

Handling complexity is not only key to successfully navigating modern business challenges, but also to drawing the right conclusions from your data. This chapter discusses complex relationships where one thing influences the relationship between two other things (moderation) or where the relationship between two things is explained by another thing (mediation).

Chapter 5: Segmenting the world

One of the key applications of analytics and even machine learning is to come up with segments or groups of elements, such as customers, products or job candidates. One key method to come up with such groups is called cluster analysis. This chapter shows you step by step how data can be used to create groups based on similarity and what similarity really means in the data context.

Chapter 6: Detecting data distortions

Even if you have followed all our guidelines in Chapters 1–5, you may still be using analytics in a wrong (or even unethical) way. Biases in your data collection, analysis or communication may be to blame for that. This chapter will thus help you immunise your analytics efforts against distortions in your data and assist you in de-biasing your data interpretation and communication.

Part 2: Communicating data

Chapter 7: Asking the right questions about data

Discussions are the catalytic element for better data use. And the basis for good discussions are great questions. This chapter gives you a mini guide for analytics Q&A sessions and shows you the main types of questions that you need to ask whenever data is presented to you.

Chapter 8: How to visually design your data

There is simply too much data to read it all. Thus, visualising data in a concise and fitting format is an essential skill for anyone working with data. This chapter gives you six simple and effective guidelines for high-quality charts. The DESIGN acronym in this chapter summarises the most important rules for visualising data. This is complemented with examples and pointers to further resources on designing great charts.

Chapter 9: The data storytelling canvas

This entertaining little chapter shows you the five magic ingredients of good data stories. They will help you make data more compelling, clear and convincing. Based on this chapter, you will know how to connect data to your audience, how to sequence data presentations and what role you play in all of this.

Chapter 10: Working with analytics software in front of others

When communicating analytics, it is becoming more frequent to ditch static presentation slides and use analytics software instead, so that the data can be explored together and that you can react to spontaneous questions. Whenever you are showing data with the help of software, there are certain caveats that you need to keep in mind. They are discussed in this chapter.

Chapter 11: Delivering bad news with data

This chapter makes a case that data that signals 'bad news' can be a powerful catalyst for improvement and progress. We offer practical communication strategies to convey bad data-based news so that you can avoid confusion, overcome resistance and turn frustration into motivation.

Chapter 12: Handling data disagreements

This chapter deals with another difficult data situation, namely when there are radically different views about data or its analysis, interpretation or use. How can you make productive use of such data controversies? Find out in this chapter and learn how to have good analytics fights that help make better data-based decisions.

Chapter 13: What's next? Sustaining your data fluency

The final chapter of the book not only sheds light on important trends that you need to monitor to keep up your data fluency, but also suggests effective ways in which you can continue to hone your analytics skills.

How each chapter is organised

We have given a preview of what's to come in terms of *content*, now let's just spend a minute on the *format* of the book. We've tried to make the subjects as accessible and entertaining as possible. That is why you will find frequent examples, boxes and diagrams throughout the book. Here are some of the recurring features of each chapter that will help you get the most out of its contents:

What you'll learn: Each chapter begins with a concise overview of its main contents and benefits to you. In this way you can better decide if and when to read each chapter. You'll also know what to expect in terms of difficulty.

Key concepts: This recurring handy diagram helps you to get a visual overview of the key concepts discussed in each chapter. It's a sort of advanced organiser and recap tool to synthesise what you need to remember from the chapter (so it will typically be placed in the first part of each chapter). You have already seen the first example of this when we gave you an overview of the concept of data fluency at the start of this introduction (see Figure 1 above). The main concept is placed in the box in the middle, while related or similar concepts can be found on the left. The top box on the right always indicates the level of difficulty of the concept, so whether it's really basic knowledge, or if it represents an advanced topic. One level down you always find a concise definition of the concept, followed by its individual components and examples thereof. Each concept snapshot finishes with action implications in its lowest section.

Data conversation: Each chapter contains a two-part data dialogue (initially gone wrong) to illustrate the challenges discussed in the chapter. At the end of each chapter, you will find a continuation of that same conversation. In this concluding part of the dialogue, the challenges are addressed with the lessons learned from the chapter.

How to say it: These short sections give you practical communication advice on how to make data more relatable to others. It also includes tips on what to avoid when collaborating with others around data.

Each chapter ends with the *key take-aways* and the *traps* to keep in mind whenever you're working with data.

So, there you have it, your guide to data fluency. Each journey begins with a first step. You have taken that step and are ready to continue. Before we dive into the key concepts of statistics, we want to present just a short chapter on why people sometimes dislike statistics and are at times even scared of data. Understanding this problem will help you become better in dealing not just with data, but also with people who don't like to work with it. Let's understand analytics anxiety first, and then fix it by explaining statistics in a clear and accessible way.

Part

1

Understanding data

Chapter

1

How to improve your data fluency: Overcome your analytics anxiety

What you'll learn

In this short chapter we will introduce the notion of analytics anxiety as a major barrier to talking about data in a constructive way in organisations. You will learn about the main components of analytics anxiety and how to overcome it. This prepares the ground for the following chapters.

Data conversation

Josh: Shall we ask your new data analyst, Eric, to come in and brief us about our risk exposure?

Steve: Uhm, this guy speaks gibberish, I'm sorry. Why don't we connect him with my assistant Gill and let her report to me the essentials then?

Josh: But Steve, I think you can really gain more insights by interacting directly with him. There are some nuances regarding our risk constellation that his cluster analysis has brought to light.

Steve: Yeah but I'm not really a quant. Let Gill crunch the numbers with him and get me the so-what, okay?

Josh: As you wish Steve, but eventually you will need to ramp up your game, you know. Even the CEO said we're on our way to a data culture in our company.

A new era of analytics has dawned and every manager and professional is now expected to be able to make *evidence-based decisions*, using the latest analytics tools and techniques.

Whether you work in sales and marketing, communication, controlling, strategy, HR, risk management, R&D or project management, data has become the new oil and no one can afford to ignore it or use it inadequately.

There's just one problem: not everybody is a rocket scientist.

We are not all highly data literate or well versed in sophisticated statistical procedures. Consequently, we may suffer from what we call *analytics anxiety*. In the following, we would like to introduce you to this crucial and timely concept, show why it matters, how it comes about and what you can do to reduce it when *working with data in organisations* (see Figure 1.1 for an overview on what's to come in this chapter).

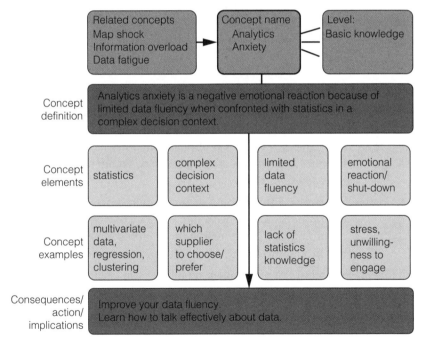

Figure 1.1 Analytics anxiety and its key components.

What is analytics anxiety?

We define analytics anxiety as feelings of fear, distress or uncertainty associated with the collection, analysis, presentation, interpretation and use of quantitative data in organisations. Analytics anxiety hence includes any feeling of distress during the process of data collection, analysis and especially communication in presentations, reports or dashboards.

Why should you care?

Analytics anxiety can severely hurt the quality of decision making and negatively influence job satisfaction. It can contribute to burnout and may cause unnecessary conflicts in management teams.

Managers and professionals who experience analytics anxiety are less likely to engage with complex data and may rely too much on their prior experiences, biases, fake news or on anecdotal evidence.

So, if you care about *decision quality*, and making evidence-based instead of eminence- or eloquence-based decisions, then you should care about analytics anxiety.

You should care about this phenomenon if you're a *professional* relying on data for decision making. If you want others to learn from your data and analyses, then you should know about analytics anxiety and what causes it, as well as effective remedies. Which brings us to our next section . . .

What causes and what reduces analytics anxiety?

Having conducted dozens of courses and training on analytics for both managers and analysts, here's what we have come to learn about the root causes and about effective solutions to this challenge.

In terms of underlying drivers of analytics anxiety affecting professionals and managers, we have identified the following seven motives for shying away from data or short-cutting one's own analytic reasoning and data deep dives:

1. **Stat phobia** – the fear of not being able to understand or interpret data correctly because of a lack of statistical understanding.

2. **Chart shock** – being cognitively and motivationally overwhelmed by the visual complexity inherent in interactive dashboards and visual analytics.

3. **Data quality paranoia** – an uneasy feeling regarding the data quality (i.e., reliability, timeliness, consistency) on which the analytics is based.

4. **Data scepticism** – the feeling that the data on its own is an insufficient base for taking a decision and that intuition and experiences should be taken into account as well.

5. **Black box allergy** – distrust in the opaque inference processes associated with data analysis, whether human-assisted or artificial-intelligence based.

6. **Incompetence compensation competence** – the reluctance to admit (in front of others) that one does not fully grasp the presented analytics. Consequently, managers only address the part of the data that they understand and neglect more difficult analytics elements.

7. **Data fatigue** – the state of being cognitively or emotionally overloaded when being presented with too much data to process in a given time period.

To address these important issues, both decision makers and data presenters have a job to do. In a nutshell, we suggest the following remedies to the analytics anxiety pandemic:

For decision makers:

1. Invest in your data fluency. Read this book carefully. Pay special attention to the chapter on analytics Q&A, but also try to understand the key take-aways from the chapters on understanding data and statistics.

2. Get reverse mentoring from younger or more well-versed colleagues who can give you a tour through analytics applications such as Tableau, RapidMiner, SAS or Power BI.

3. Oblige your analysts to pre-structure their results in categories that you're familiar with. Also, ask them to focus their analysis on the data that is really crucial for your decisions (to avoid chart shock or data fatigue). Tell them about proven data communication practices, such as those in the chapter on data visualisation and design and the one on the five magic ingredients of data storytelling.

4. Admit when you don't understand a data set or statistical procedure. You're setting an example for others and hence helping steer conversations away from pseudo understanding to greater clarity.

For those of you who are presenting data:

1. Boost your analytics *communication* skills and learn which mistakes analysts and data scientists are most likely to make and should avoid (such as providing details without overview or focusing on methodology first instead of why and for whom the data matters).

2. Respect the key *visualisation guidelines* when showing your analytics results graphically (such as never using pie charts or stacked bar charts as they are perceptually inefficient). Check out the data visualisation and design chapter in this book.

3. Combine big data with *big knowledge* by representing your numeric analyses side-by-side with knowledge visualisations which illustrate qualitative insights in overview.

4. Use the power of data *storytelling* to make your data more easily understandable and engaging. Use our data storytelling chapter to prepare and design your data presentations. In doing so, pay attention to first achieve *common ground* with your audience (front-load examples) and then clarify the situation, complications and resolution through your data. Close your data presentation with a concise call to action – if possible.

Data conversation (continued)

Steve: So, Gill did you have a chance to talk to that Eric guy about our risk exposure?

Gill: Yes, I did, and he really had amazing insights for us on where we are exposed to risks, and more importantly, how to reduce our risk exposure. We have to be mindful of the assumptions underlying the cluster analysis that he did though.

Steve: What do you mean?

▶

9

Gill:	Well, the way he grouped our risks is one way, but I think we need a less granular approach for our context to keep it efficient for decision making.
Steve:	So, the cluster analysis did not reveal a clear-cut risk grouping?
Gill:	Of course not, it gives us just the similarity metrics among all of our documented risks and various ways of grouping them. But you know that's how clustering works, right?
Steve:	Ehem, sorta.
Gill:	Here's the dendrogram, where would you cut off the groups (shows him a complex looking chart)?
Steve:	Um, I have no clue.
Gill:	I thought you could provide some input based on your strategic outlook on risks. Combined with this data-driven chart, that would really be the ideal combination and help us devise a risk segmentation and corresponding measures.
Steve:	I guess I'll have a look at this cluster analysis thing first and then get back to you.
Gill:	Let's do that, why not have Eric on board for that discussion, I think it will help combine all of our insights together.
Steve:	Okay, let's try this.
Gill:	In fact, why don't we let him walk us step-by-step through the cluster analysis. This way we can combine learning the method and learning about our risk data.
Steve:	Okay, deal.

Key take-aways

If an organisation wants to profit from the data it gathers for better decision making and opportunity detection, then it must address the issue of analytics anxiety. Simply hoping that people will interact seamlessly around data is naïve.

Real efforts need to be undertaken on both sides to improve this important interface between in-depth data expertise and managerial decision power. Academic research has an important role to play in this optimisation effort. HR professionals should study to what extent analytics anxiety exists, what its main drivers are, and which measures best reduce it. They can then transform their findings into management, consultant and analyst training. Together, these groups can take the anxiety out of analytics.

 Traps

The key risks regarding analytics anxiety are:

- Making decisions based on an inadequate understanding of relevant data.
- Shying away from important in-depth discussion with data scientists about essential business opportunities.
- Making people look foolish when they ask honest questions about analytics procedures.
- Establishing a confrontational relationship among data analysts and business professionals instead of a collaborative one.

Further resources

To quiz yourself on your current data fluency, use one of these websites and their short tests:

https://quizlet.com/435307132/data-fluency-quizzes-flash-cards/

https://thedataliteracyproject.org/assessment

https://newslit.org/tips-tools/can-you-make-sense-of-data/

Chapter

Making sense of statistics: Achieving an overall view of your data

What you'll learn

In this chapter, we give you the basic concepts and vocabulary that you need to understand and talk competently about data. You will learn how to gain an overview of your data by looking at so-called 'frequency distributions' – basically an answer to the question: 'How much of what is there?'. This will help you get a quick but solid understanding of your data and the trends that they may reveal.

Data conversation

'The results from a recent survey among our ten most important business customers are really worrying me', said Jim, while nervously playing with his pencil. 'We asked them to indicate how satisfied they are with our customer relationship management and, on average, they gave us a rating of just 6.8 out of 10 points. This is considerably worse than last year where we received a rating of 8.5', he continued.

Jim joined the customer relationship team only six months ago, thus he felt uncomfortable delivering bad news – particularly because the head of customer relationship management attended the meeting.

▶

His team members all looked a bit confused. They thought they had done a good job and they couldn't understand why they didn't get a better rating.

No one said anything, until one of the team members, Lisa, raised her hand and asked: 'Are there any *outliers*?' Jim was a bit perplexed and replied that he hadn't checked for outliers and that he didn't know why he should. 'Well, it might help us to better understand this result and maybe it shows that things aren't as bad as they look', she explained. After a short discussion, the team agreed that Jim should take a look at the results again and look for outlier cases.

Intuition and experience are important pillars in professional life. However, with the world becoming ever more complex, volatile and dynamic, relying on intuition and experience alone can be risky and result in bad decisions.

Sometimes our intuition tricks us and sometimes even the most experienced managers must come to realise that things work differently than they thought. And being wrong can come at high costs. Being wrong can mean that sales shrink, customers quit or, in the worst case, that people die. And that's where data come into play.

Statistics is *the* key to make your data speak. Statistics allows you to decipher your data and discover the story they tell. But why should you invest your time in engaging with statistics when you have data analysts in your organisation whose job it is to squeeze the answers to your questions out of your data?

The answer is simple: having a basic knowledge of statistics helps you to fully exploit the insights from the data analyses and draw the right conclusions. Perhaps, even more importantly, it helps you understand whether the statistical models that were used really fit the purpose. Otherwise, you may get answers to questions that you never asked.

So let's get started by understanding the *types* of data that we need to deal with in business and why Jim should carefully look at outliers before making generalisations.

Statistics is used to analyse all kinds of data that involve numbers. These data are called **quantitative data**. They are objective and measurable. Quantitative data help to quantify a phenomenon and to answer questions such as 'what are our best-selling products?', 'how much money did people donate to our charity?' or 'how many employees have quit their job in our company in the last six months?'.

Quantitative data can be obtained, for instance, through surveys, experiments, or metrics (like website users' online behaviour or your accounting system).

If your data do not involve numbers, then they are called **qualitative data**. They are subjective and filled with personal views. Qualitative data give us more detail and context and answer questions such as 'why do people buy our products?' or 'how come that we have difficulties recruiting volunteers?'. Qualitative data can be gathered through focus groups, observations or text documents, just to name a few.

When we talk about data analysis in this book, we refer to the analysis of quantitative data.

In the modern working world, numbers in the form of quantitative data have moved to the forefront of decision making. Some might even say that business has developed a bit of an obsession with quantitative data. Everything seems to be counted, measured and put into numbers (whether it makes sense or not). However, before we can start with crunching numbers, we need to know how we can obtain quantitative data. How do we get all the numbers? And what are the different types of data we can collect and use for our decision making?

Quantitative data are measured by **variables**. You can imagine variables as kitchen vessels and data as the things that are inside. Each vessel contains things *of the same kind*. For instance, one bowl contains salad and the other apples. Within each bowl, there may be a certain variation. The salad leaves may differ in their size and the apples in their roundness. In other words: variables capture things of the same kind that can change and take different values. People, for example, can vary regarding their age, their consumption preferences, their propensity to volunteer, or their donation or purchasing behaviours. Similarly, organisations can vary by their size, their resources, or their social impact. Likewise, nations can vary in their political system or their official languages. Moreover, things can change over time (e.g., people's mood, income, or health; organisational growth; a nation's economic stability).

We can distinguish variables based on how they can be measured. Why is that important? Because it determines what you can do with these variables. Using inappropriate or even wrong statistical methods leads to bad decisions.

Figure 2.1 gives you an overview of the different types of variables and in Figure 2.2 you can find a practical example for each of the variable types.

Variables can be classified as either categorical or continuous (Cramer and Howitt, 2004). A **categorical variable**, as the name implies, is one that consists of categories. These categories are mutually exclusive so that an object only falls into one of these categories. Categorical variables you might be familiar with are organisation type (for-profit, non-governmental, public) or type of donation (money, services, goods, blood, organs etc.). In its simplest form, a categorical variable is made up of two categories. Such

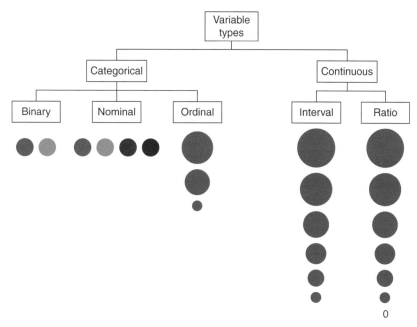

Figure 2.1 An overview of different variable types.

variables are called **binary variables**. Examples of binary variables are being a client or not; having the lead in a project or not; and being a minor or not.

If a variable contains more than two categories such as nationality (American, British, French, Spanish, German, Swiss etc.) or job location (London, New York, Zurich etc.), then we speak of a **nominal variable**. The categories of binary and nominal variables are unordered. That means, we consider them as equal. When the categories are ordered, we have an **ordinal variable**. Examples include educational level (elementary school, high school, higher education) or job title (employee, manager, director, chief operating officer etc.). Also, when a humanitarian organisation asks beneficiaries about their health and they can answer 'very bad', 'somewhat bad', 'neutral', 'somewhat good' or 'very good', you have an ordinal variable. However, while we can rank these answers, we cannot tell anything about the differences between the values. We cannot say, for instance, that 'neutral' is twice as good as 'somewhat bad'.

If we want to say something about the differences between the values, we need **continuous variables**. Continuous variables can take the form of interval or ratio variables.

An **interval variable** is one where the difference between any two values is meaningful. Let's say an organisation conducts a survey among its employees. The employees would be asked to report their job satisfaction with their work on a seven-point scale ranging from 1 (not satisfied at all) to 7 (very satisfied). The differences between any two values are meaningful because the intervals are equal (e.g., the differences are equal between 1 and 2 or between 5 and 6).

Ratio variables not only require equal distances between any two values but also a 'natural' zero point. For instance, the number of strategic projects completed is a ratio variable as it has a meaningful zero point: 0 means that someone has not yet completed a strategic project and 5 means that someone has already completed five strategic projects.

Interval and ratio variables can be **discrete or 'truly continuous'** (Field, 2018). Discrete means that a variable can only take specific values (usually whole numbers). The number of strategic projects completed is an example of a discrete variable – you may have completed one, two, three, six or eight, projects but not 3.4 or 5.2 projects. Continuous means that the variable can take an infinite number of values within a range of values. A typical example is the exact weight or height of a person (e.g., someone can be 1.7224353636 m tall).

You now understand that there are different types of variables and that these can be distinguished based on their levels of measurement. To further clarify the different types of variables, Figure 2.2 provides an example.

Categorical Variables

- Binary: Project lead (0 = project member vs 1 = project leader) ☐

- Nominal: Workplace (1 = London, 2 = New York, 3 = Zurich) ◼

- Ordinal: Job title (1 = Manager, 2 = Director, 3 = Chief Operating Officer) ◼

Continuous Variables

- Interval: Job satisfaction (1: not satisfied at all to 7: very satisfied)

- Ratio: Number of strategic projects completed (0 − X)

Figure 2.2 Examples of different variable types from a business context.

⚠ **How to say it**

Spell out variable names

Time is precious and to communicate as efficiently as possible we often use abbreviations and acronyms. When talking about variables, it has become common place to employ abbreviations (e.g., Att. = attitude; Beh. = behaviours) and acronyms (e.g., ASPM = average sales per month). But caution is warranted when doing so. Such labels may be clear and easy-to-understand for those who are familiar with a topic or a data set (experts), but not to the rest (novices). Using abbreviations and acronyms for variable names often causes confusion among novice audiences and makes it hard for them to follow the analysis or the conclusions drawn. To avoid imposing unnecessary stress on audiences and scaring them off, spell out variable names whenever possible, i.e., briefly mention what an acronym means and put the explanation on your slides or reports as well. Ask your data scientists to explain the acronyms that they are using, especially if you feel that other audience members are too shy to ask about this.

So now that you have seen the different kinds of data, what can we do with them?

Often, we are interested in the *relationship* between variables. We might want to know whether people's income influences the amount of charitable donations that they make or whether monetary incentives increase your employees' performance. Such relationships can be expressed in terms of two types of variables: **predictors** and **outcomes** (Field, 2018).

Taking the example from above, income would be the predictor and the amount of charitable donations would be the outcome. Likewise, incentives would be thought to predict job performance.

Sometimes predictors are also referred to as **independent variables** and outcomes as **dependent variables**. Be careful with these terms though. Strictly speaking, you should only speak of independent and dependent variables when the proposed cause was manipulated (that means directly influenced or modified). For instance, you could be interested in whether the type of Facebook posting predicts the number of likes. You may make a posting with an appealing image that shows the impact of your humanitarian work and compare it to a posting that only verbally describes the impact of your humanitarian work. Then, you could measure the number of likes for each posting. Because you actively manipulated – or changed – the type of Facebook posting you can refer to it as a predictor or independent variable and you can refer to the number of likes as an outcome or dependent variable. However, in case you are not sure whether the predictor was manipulated or not, just stay with the predictor/outcome terminology.

⚠ How to say it

Call the child by its name

Managers often tell us anecdotes about their colleagues or data analysts using overly complex and technical vocabulary. 'It is as if they were talking in another language', a manager reported jokingly in one of our workshops. To keep your audience interested and focused during your data presentations (and to avoid that their thoughts wander off to their next holiday trips, their most urgent to-dos, or their plans for dinner), it is important to use clear, concrete (example-driven) and concise language. It may be hard to follow your analysis when you say something like 'a predictor had a significant impact on the outcome'. Instead, be *specific* about what you mean. Tell your audience that the number of food packages that were distributed (predictor) significantly increased the well-being of the beneficiaries (outcome) or that the amount of advertising spending (predictor) positively impacted product sales (outcome).

So far, we have been concerned with the types of variables (i.e., categorical vs continuous) and their function in relationships (predictor vs outcome). As you will see in the following pages, these distinctions are key to statistics literacy. They provide you with a robust foundation to analyse data and choose *appropriate and informative measures*. Keep in mind that you always gather and analyse data with a specific purpose in mind (except if you belong to the rare group of people who engage with data just for the fun of it). Thus, make sure that the measures you choose are suitable for your goals and help you make good decisions.

Figure 2.3 gives an overview of the basics that you need to know to get an overview and a feel for your data. This is crucial because in a world where everything needs to be done immediately and where we are running from meeting to meeting, time is money. And so is knowledge of how to get a quick but solid understanding of your data and the trends that they may reveal.

Imagine that you just received data on the success of an important strategic project. You open the file, see all the numbers, and feel your heart pound faster and your hands getting sweaty. You burn to learn what the data will tell you, but you don't know where to start.

An easy and quick way to get an overview of your data and a feel for trends – provided there are any – is to construct **frequency distributions** (Figure 2.3). Frequency distributions show how often each value occurs in your data set (Field, 2018). Frequency distributions can be presented using different *formats*: tables and graphs. Let's assume that your team has collected data about how long volunteers have been working for your organisation (ratio variable: length of volunteering in years) and you now want to see how the values are distributed. You can organise the data into a table. As you can see in the table in Figure 2.4, the data indicate that 29 volunteers have served your organisation for 5 years, whereas only one has been in your organisation for 9 years. Likewise, you can organise the data in a graphical representation (Figure 2.4). This can be easily done with data visualisation tools such as Tableau. When visualised as graphs, frequency distributions can take the form of histograms or bar charts. The y-axis represents the frequency count and the x-axis represents the variable of interest. The graph contains the same information as the table, but in visual form. Histograms are often preferred to tables as they allow for a more comprehensive and richer overview – particularly when you have large data sets and many different values per variable.

Frequency distributions are a bit like buildings: they take many different shapes and sizes. Therefore, having a vocabulary to describe

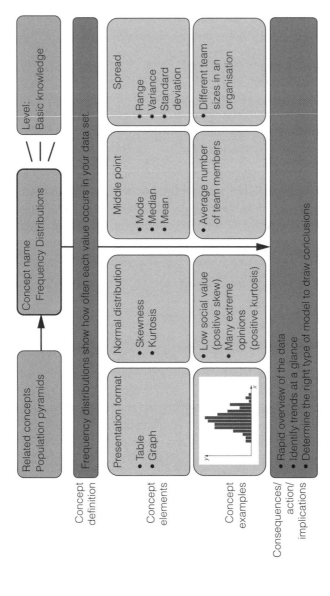

Figure 2.3 The concept of frequency distributions and its components.

Length of volunteering in years	Frequency	Per cent
2	4	4
3	9	9
4	24	24
5	29	29
6	19	19
7	11	11
8	3	3
9	1	1
Total	100	100

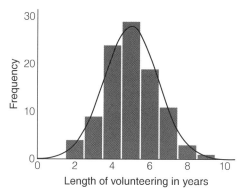

Figure 2.4 Frequency distributions can be presented using tables (left) or using visualisations (right).

these types of distributions is crucial for anyone involved with data. Distributions are most commonly described in terms of how much they deviate from a normal distribution (Field, 2018). You may not have heard about **normal distributions** (also known as Gaussian distributions), but you have surely seen them. A normal distribution forms a bell curve and is symmetrical: if we fold it in the middle, the two sides look completely the same. Normal distributions are too perfect to be true you may think. But surprise, surprise, they can be found anywhere: lots of natural and man-made phenomena are normally distributed. For instance, height, IQ, or marks on a test are commonly observed to follow a normal distribution. Look at the histogram in Figure 2.4 again: the black line represents the normal curve. As you can see, the length of volunteering in this organisation is nearly normally distributed. The nearer you come to the centre – or the middle – of the distribution, the more values you have. That means that there are many values in the centre and only a few values on the tails.

Distributions can deviate from normal in the following two ways: (1) lack of symmetry (**skewness**) and (2) pointiness (**kurtosis**). Skewed distributions are not symmetrical because the most frequently observed values cluster at one end of the distribution and not in the centre of the distribution (Field, 2018). A positively skewed distribution means that the most frequent values are clustered at the lower end of the distribution, whereas a negatively skewed distribution means that the most frequent values are clustered at the upper end of the distribution (Figure 2.5).

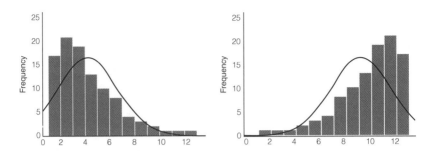

Figure 2.5 Positively skewed distribution (left) and negatively skewed distribution (right).

Kurtosis tells us something about how pointy a distribution is. It describes the degree to which values cluster at the ends – also referred to as the tails – of a distribution (Field, 2018). Distributions with positive kurtosis have many values in the tails and many values close to the centre. This is what makes them look pointy. The opposite applies to distributions with negative kurtosis. Here you have fewer values in the tails and fewer values close to the centre. The curve looks flat because it has more dispersed values with lighter tails (Figure 2.6). Skewness and kurtosis statistics can give you helpful insights about your data. Let's assume you wanted to rate your attractiveness as an employer using different questions measured on a scale from 1 (to a very little extent) to 7 (to a very

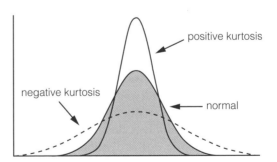

Figure 2.6 Distribution with normal, positive kurtosis and negative kurtosis.

great extent) (Sivertzen *et al.*, 2013). If the analysis shows that your employees' responses about the social value of your organisation (i.e., whether your organisation offers a positive and pleasant social environment) have a heavy positive skew, you should probably be alerted. It means that your employees most frequently rated your organisation as having a low social value. Similarly, the data on the interest value of your organisation (i.e., whether your organisation offers interesting and stimulating jobs) might exhibit a positive kurtosis. This means that you have more extreme values than if the data were normally distributed. Specifically, there is a greater amount of people who either find their jobs very interesting or very uninteresting (i.e., many scores in the tails).

After having an overview of how your values are distributed, you may want to find out where the centre of the distribution lies. Measures of **central tendency** (also known as **central location**) are summary statistics that locate the middle point or typical value of a distribution. It is important to know about the measures of central tendency because they help you describe your data with a single value (Porkess and Goldie, 2012). However, failure to choose the right – or most appropriate – measure of central tendency can give you a distorted or misleading impression of your data. The three most commonly used measures are: the mode, the median and the mean (Cramer and Howitt, 2004).

The **mode** is the value that occurs most often in your data set (Field, 2018). The mode is easy to find in a histogram because it is the tallest bar. The two bar charts in Figure 2.7 show how often the members of a sports association have made a donation in the last ten years. In the chart on the left, the mode is 5 because it is

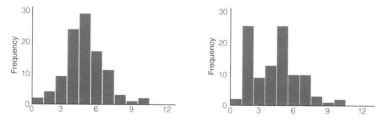

Figure 2.7 Distribution with one mode (left) and distribution with two modes (right).

the value that occurs most often. It means that the most frequent number of donations is five. But as illustrated in Figure 2.7, some distributions have more than one mode. A distribution with two modes is called a **bimodal distribution** and a distribution with more than two modes is known as **multimodal distribution**. The mode is the measure of central tendency that can be used for categorical and continuous variables (provided that they have discrete values).

The mode, although easy to calculate and comprehend, has several downsides. First, when each value only occurs once, there is no mode. Second, the mode may provide an inaccurate description of your data because it does not consider all values (it only considers the most frequently observed value and ignores all other values). The following two charts (Figure 2.8) illustrate this point. As you can see in the graph on the right, the mode does not accurately locate the central tendency when the most frequently observed value is far away from the rest of the values.

The **median** is the value that splits the data into two halves. You can find the median by ordering your data from smallest to largest. The median is the value in the middle that has an equal number of values below and above it (Field, 2018). Imagine going around in your organisation and asking 11 team leaders from different divisions about the size of their team. You note the following number of team members for these 11 managers: 3, 15, 7, 2, 10, 5, 6, 8, 11, 13, 4. To calculate the median, you first need to sort these values into ascending order: 2, 3, 4, 5, 6, 7, 8, 10, 11, 13, 15.

In a next step, you count the number of scores (n), add 1 to this value, and then divide it by 2.

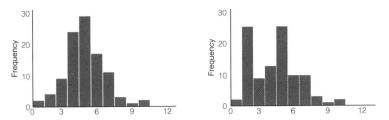

Figure 2.8 Mode accurately locates the middle of the distribution (left) versus mode does not accurately locate the middle of the distribution (right).

Equation: Median odd

$$\frac{(n+1)}{2} = \frac{(11+1)}{2} = \frac{12}{2} = 6$$

where n is the number of values.

This indicates to us that the sixth value is the middle value of this distribution. We thus know that the median is 7 team members. Calculating the median is straightforward when you have an odd number of values. But what happens when you have an even number of values (Figure 2.9)? What if you asked 12 managers about the size of their team? Let's say this twelfth team leader has 9 people in her team. This would mean that the median is halfway between the sixth and the seventh value (Equation: Median even). To get the median, we just add the sixth and the seventh value and divide this value by 2. Hence, the median number of team members would be 7.5. Figure 2.9 visually summarises the calculations for the median.

Equation: Median even

$$\frac{(n+1)}{2} = \frac{(12+1)}{2} = \frac{13}{2} = 6.5$$

where n is the number of values.

The median can be used with ordinal, interval and ratio variables. We cannot use it with binary or categorical variables because the categories are considered equal and therefore unordered. The median is similar to the mode in that both ignore most values in the data set. The median only considers the value(s) in the middle of the distribution and does not consider all information available in the data. However, the median is relatively robust and less distorted by skewed data and outliers than the mean (Field, 2018).

Probably the most popular and known measure of central tendency is the **mean**. The concept behind the mean is quite simple, although the equation may look cumbersome. You basically just add up all the values and then divide the sum by the number of values that you have. The symbol $\bar{x}$ stands for the mean, Σ is the Greek letter Sigma and tells you to sum up all values (x) and n represents the number of values you have. In our example with the 12 managers the mean is 7.75. That signifies that, on average, the managers have 7.75 team members.

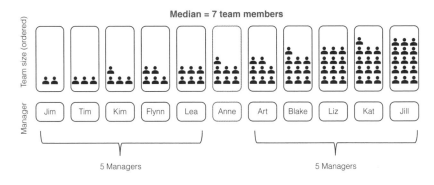

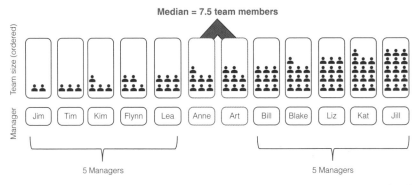

Figure 2.9 How to calculate the median with an odd number of cases (top) versus with an even number of cases (bottom).

Equation: Mean

$$\bar{x} = \frac{\sum_{i=1}^{n} x_i}{n}$$

where $\bar{x}$ represents the mean, $\sum$ means sum up, n denotes the number of values, x_i means the ith value of x.

Equation: Mean (example)

$$\frac{2 + 3 + 4 + 5 + 6 + 7 + 8 + 9 + 10 + 11 + 13 + 15}{12} = 7.75$$

The mean can only be calculated with interval or ratio variables. Moreover, the mean has two major disadvantages: it can be influenced by skewed data and outliers. As the data becomes skewed, the mean loses its ability to represent the most typical value in the data set because the skewed data is dragging it away from the centre (Field, 2018). Look again at Figure 2.5 and try to imagine how skewness affects the mean. **Outliers** are extreme values in that they are very different from the other values in the data set (Field, 2018). Because the mean considers *all* values, one or a few extreme values can heavily distort it (see dialogue box). When you have outliers and/or skewed data, it is recommended to use the median instead of the mean (remember: the median is more robust).

Data conversation (continued)

The follow-up meeting on the results of the B2B (business to business) customer survey was scheduled for the next day.

Jim carefully looked at the data again to get an idea about outliers and the measures of central tendency.

At the start of the meeting Jim said 'I found an interesting pattern', and passed a sheet with two charts to his colleagues (see below). 'It seems that the majority of our B2B customers is in fact happy with our customer relationship management. Most B2B customers, except for two, gave us very good ratings', Jim argued.

His colleagues and his boss were intrigued as Jim could tell by the way they examined the sheet.

'Oh, I think I know what happened. Remember this very inconvenient misunderstanding we had with two large B2B customers? That was just a few days before we sent out the survey. That probably affected their response', one of the team members mentioned. Everyone knew about this incident and they were happy that they had been able to straighten things out and clarify the misunderstanding in the meanwhile. 'Well done, Jim. We should definitely include this graph in our report to the director', the head of customer relationship management said. 'We can write a comment on these two outliers and explain why they probably gave us such a poor rating. We can show that these outliers heavily impact the mean and that the median is more robust and more representative

▶

of our data', she elaborated. After the meeting, Jim went back to his office. He was happy because not only had he learnt something new about statistics, he had also helped his team to better understand the results of the survey.

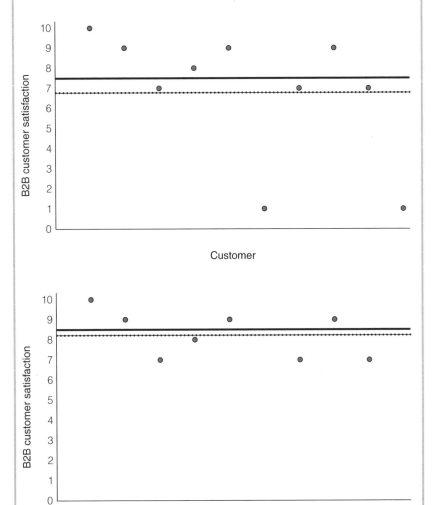

Upper graph: mean (dotted line) and median (the other line) when outliers are included. Lower graph: mean (dotted line) and median (the other line) when outliers are excluded.

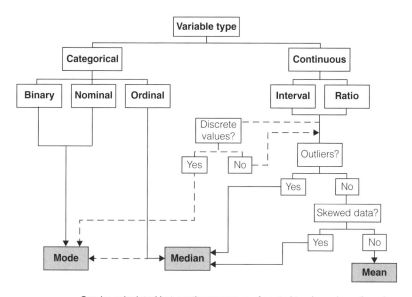

 Can be calculated but another measure of central tendency is preferred

Figure 2.10 How to choose an appropriate measure of central tendency.

We have learnt that the mode, the median and the mean are the most commonly used measures to determine the middle point of a distribution. However, each measure comes with advantages and disadvantages. Moreover, some measures only work for specific variable types. So, the question is what measure of central tendency to use? The decision tree above helps you choose an appropriate measure (Figure 2.10).

⚠️ **How to say it**

The thing with the average

When people speak of the 'average', they are often referring to the 'mean'. But as you can see, there are several types of averages, with the most commonly used being the mode, median, and mean. Thus, to avoid misunderstandings, always make explicit what measure(s) of central tendency you are using and why. Also, you may want to make people aware of the limitations of the mean and point them to other factors in a data set, such as the variance. This is further discussed in the next section.

How different is my data? A deviant tale about range

Locating the middle of the distribution is one thing, but the other important point is to identify the **spread**, or **dispersion**, of the values (Porkess and Goldie, 2012). The spread tells you how scattered the data is. This is important to know because it gives us an idea of how informative or reliable the measures of central tendency are. Put differently: the spread gives us an idea of how well the measures of central tendency represent the data. If the spread of values is large, the measures of central tendency are less representative of the data than if the spread of values is small. Therefore, we want the spread to be small. Let's illustrate this with an example. Imagine you were the leader of a sales team and you saw that, on average, your team sold 1,000 cars per year over the last 15 years. The mean value of 1,000 cars, however, is not really informative when the number of cars sold varies largely between the years – for instance, when your team sold 50 or 60 cars in some years and 5,000 cars in other years.

The **range** is the easiest measure of dispersion (Figure 2.11). You can calculate the range by taking the largest value in your data and subtract it from the smallest value (Field, 2018). Imagine you obtained information about how many projects your seven top managers have initiated within the last 12 months. If you order these data, you get 1, 2, 4, 5, 7, 9, 11. As you can see, the highest value is 11 and the lowest value is 1. The range is accordingly $11 - 1 = 10$. Because the range is based on two extreme observations (i.e., highest and smallest value), it is heavily affected by outliers.

A common workaround to this problem is to calculate the **interquartile range**. That means, you cut off the top and bottom 25% of values and calculate the range between the middle 50% of values (Field, 2018). For our project data, the interquartile range would be $9 - 2 = 7$ (see Figure 2.12).

The interquartile range is not susceptible to outliers, but that comes at high costs. We lose a lot of data. Just as in real life, there are things of which we might want to get rid: weight, debts and/or bad

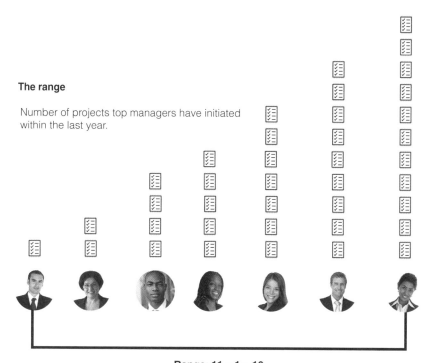

The range

Number of projects top managers have initiated within the last year.

Range: 11 − 1 = 10

Figure 2.11 Calculating the range.

habits. But commonly, we don't want to lose things because we need them (or feel that we need them). With data, it's similar. In most cases, we try to keep them and consider them in our analyses.

If we want to determine the spread of our data including all values, we can look at how far away each value is from the middle of the distribution. This gives us a more encompassing and holistic understanding of our data. If we use the mean as the middle point of the distribution, we can calculate the **deviation.** This is the difference between each value and the mean (Field, 2018).

Equation: Deviation

$$\text{Deviation} = (x_i - \bar{x})$$

where x_i means the ith value of x and $\bar{x}$ represents the mean.

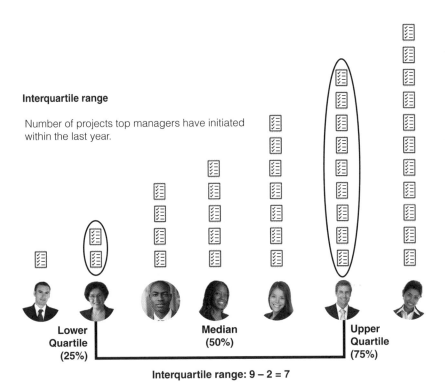

Figure 2.12 Calculating the interquartile range.

If we want to know the total deviation, then we can just add up the deviation for each value.

Equation: Total deviation

$$\text{Total deviation} = \sum_{i=1}^{n}(x_i - \bar{x})$$

where $\sum$ represents sum up, n is the number of values, x_i means the ith value of x and $\bar{x}$ represents the mean.

Let's illustrate this with our strategy project. Look at Figure 2.13. The x-axis represents the seven managers and the y-axis represents the number of projects that they have initiated. The horizontal line stands for the mean and the vertical lines stand for the differences between the mean and each value. Note that the deviations can be positive or negative (depending on whether a given value lies above or below the mean). When we add up all the deviations, however, the total is zero.

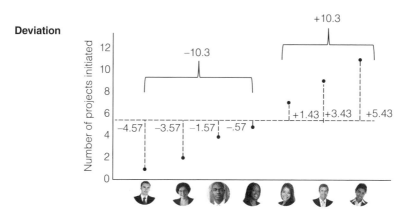

Figure 2.13 Deviation in the project.

To overcome this problem, we can use the squared deviation. All you have to do is just to square each deviation (difference between the mean and each value) and add these squared deviations together. This is what is known as the **sum of squared errors (SS)**. We can use the sum of squared errors as an indicator for the spread of our data. However, there's a 'but' here. The problem is that the total size depends on how many values we have. If we had another 40 values in our project data example, the sum of squared errors would be considerably higher. The implication is that we cannot compare the sum of squared errors across groups that differ in size. What we want is a measure of dispersion that is not dependent on the number of values that we have.

We therefore calculate the *average dispersion*, which is also referred to as **variance**. We take the sum of squared errors and divide it by the number of values minus 1 (Field, 2018). But there's a catch: the variance provides a measure in units squared because we used the sum of *squared* errors. This makes the variance difficult to interpret. In our example, we would say that the average error was 13.3 projects initiated squared. It's obvious that this interpretation isn't very informative because it makes little sense to talk about projects initiated squared. We therefore take the square root of the variance. This really important measure is called the **standard deviation**. It's generally considered the gold standard to express how scattered the values in a data set are. If you do not want to calculate the standard deviation on your own, you can find helpful tools that will do the work for you.[1]

Equation: Variance

$$\text{Variance } (s^2) = \frac{\text{Sum of squared errors (SS)}}{N-1} = \frac{\sum_{i=1}^{n}(x_i - \bar{x})^2}{n-1}$$

where Σ represents sum up, n is the number of values, x_i means the ith value of x and $\bar{x}$ represents the mean.

Equation: Standard deviation

$$s = \sqrt{\frac{\sum_{i=1}^{n}(x_i - \bar{x})^2}{n-1}}$$

where $\sqrt{}$ is the square root, Σ represents sum up, n is the number of values, x_i means the ith value of x and $\bar{x}$ represents the mean.

The sum of squares, the variance and the standard deviations are all measures that determine the spread of data around the *mean* (Field, 2018). The smaller the spread, the closer are the data to the mean (the more similar they are). The bigger the spread, the further away are the data from the mean. Figure 2.14 compares the number of projects initiated by top managers across two non-profit organisations. Both organisations have the same average of projects initiated (mean of 5.6). However, the number of projects initiated in organisation X spreads much more than the number of projects initiated in organisation Y. This tells us that the number of projects initiated is more consistent across managers in organisation Y, whereas there are greater differences between managers in organisation X.

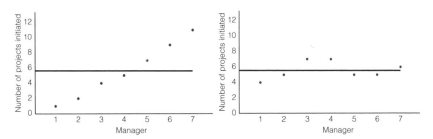

Figure 2.14 Number of initiated projects in organisation X, standard deviation = 3.6 (left) and number of initiated projects in organisation Y, standard deviation = 1.1 (right).

⚠ **How to say it**

The pitfall of being overly precise: Decimals and large numbers

Accuracy is often seen as an important indicator for data quality. However, being overly precise and accurate may produce a boomerang effect. Many people have difficulties perceiving and interpreting numbers with decimals. For instance, the following numbers are hard to digest: M (Mean) = 3.45678; SD (Standard Deviation) = 1.23987. As a rule of thumb: do not use more than one or two decimals. In specific cases, three decimal places may be adequate to show subtle differences in a distribution. This is much easier to read: M (Mean) = 3.5; SD (Standard Deviation) = 1.2.

Similarly, large numbers are difficult to read, understand and memorise. For example, 5630321 products sold looks like a lot, but it is difficult to grasp how much it actually is. In such cases, it is advisable to use rounded numbers or commas/apostrophes or spaces as a thousand separator.

Rounded numbers: 5.6 million products sold

Commas: 5,630,321 products sold

Apostrophes: 5'630'321 products sold

Spaces: 5 630 321 products sold

Key take-aways

Admittedly, most people don't burst into joy when dealing with data and statistics. However, in this chapter we have learnt that statistics is the key to make your data speak and that it can help you navigate and break down the complexity of your work environment (and hopefully you have also learnt that statistics is not as bad as its reputation and that it can actually be fun).

Whenever you are dealing with data, there are a few questions that are important to ask from a statistical point of view.

1. What kind of data do you have (quantitative vs qualitative)? And is it appropriate to analyse these data using statistics?

2. What level of measurement do the variables of interest have (categorical vs continuous)? What types of averages (i.e., measures of central tendency) are hence most appropriate (mode, median, mean)?

3. Are there outliers in your data? What are possible explanations for these extreme values? Should they be eliminated for some of the statistical analyses to avoid distorted results?

4. How does the distribution of your variables look? Does the distribution form a perfect bell curve, or does it deviate from the normal (i.e., skewness and kurtosis)?

5. How consistent are your data based on their spread?

6. When presenting data, did you make sure that you are communicating in simple and clear terms (e.g., spelling out variable names; being specific about what you mean; specifying what kind of average you are using and why; not using more than two or three decimals; rounding up large numbers or using thousand separators).

 Traps

Analytics traps

- Failure to determine the right level of measurement of your data (e.g., wrongfully classifying an ordinal variable as an interval variable, although the distances between any two values are not equal).
- Calculating the median or mean for nominal variables.
- Calculating the mean for continuous data that is heavily skewed.
- Calculating the mean for continuous data that has many outliers and not discussing the influence of these outliers.
- Comparing means without considering the spread of data.

Communication traps

- Using abbreviations and acronyms (for variable names).
- Speaking of independent and dependent variables instead of predictors and outcomes when you only *observed* things but did not *manipulate or influence* them yourself.

- Presenting frequency distributions using pie charts instead of histograms or bar charts.
- Speaking of 'averages' without specifying what kind of average you mean (e.g., mode, median or mean).
- Offering a misleading interpretation of variance by ignoring that it provides a measure in *units squared.*
- Overwhelming your audiences with more than two or three decimals and with large numbers that are not rounded up or that are not separated by thousand separators (e.g., commas, apostrophes, spaces).

Further resources

For a short video on how to create a frequency distribution:

https://www.youtube.com/watch?v=amLYLq73RvE

This online calculator calculates the mean, median, mode as well as the range and the interquartile range for you:

https://www.calculatorsoup.com/calculators/statistics/mean-median-mode.php

Note

1. https://www.calculator.net/standard-deviation-calculator.html
   https://www.statisticshowto.com/calculators/variance-and-standard-deviation-calculator/

Chapter

3

Modelling the world with data: Predicting outcomes

What you'll learn

This chapter shows you how to identify patterns in your data and understand what they mean. You will also learn how to use your data for predictive purposes (e.g., find out to what extent one thing influences another thing). Moreover, we will address what it takes to infer generalisations from data and what distinguishes 'statistically significant' from 'practically meaningful' findings.

Data conversation

For some weeks, Elaine's team members have been more stressed and thin-skinned than usual. It was like a dark cloud was hanging over their heads. That dark cloud came in the form of a competitor who had launched a new energy drink that was very similar to their own 'cash cow product'. 'Will customers like the competitor's energy drink better and thus stop buying ours?' – the team members often worried and debated this question in their coffee break. Elaine, the head of marketing, hence commissioned a market research institute to conduct a survey on customers' responses to both drinks.

It was a Monday morning, when suddenly an email from the market research institute popped up in her inbox. The institute informed Elaine that the data collection had been completed and that they had conducted a study with more than 4,000 participants. Moreover, attached to this email, they sent Elaine the raw data. Elaine was curious, opened the data file and started to explore the

▶

---

data. She had a basic knowledge in statistics and felt sufficiently confident to do the analysis herself. As Elaine ran the analysis, she became paler and paler. She printed out the analysis results, got up from her desk and walked straight into her team colleague's office. 'Barbara, you won't believe this', she said without knocking on the door. 'I just looked at the data from the market research institute. People seem to like our competitor's energy drink significantly better than ours', she said. But, hold on – maybe Elaine didn't see the full picture . . .

It is in the very nature of humans to be curious about how the world works. Maybe you touched the hot stove as a child to see what would happen (and hopefully learned your lesson) or maybe you tried out what best to say to get your crush's attention. This innate drive to figure out how things are *related* also accompanies us in our professional life. Typical questions relevant to the professional context in which you are working might be: 'How is the weather related to the sales of your product (e.g., ice cream or umbrellas)?' or 'How is the number of volunteers connected to organisational goal achievement?'. Understanding the relationship between things gives you a richer and more in-depth understanding of your projects and helps you make more informed decisions. This is exactly what is needed in this ever more complex and intricate world.

However, be aware that just because two things appear to be connected, doesn't necessarily mean that there is a cause-and-effect relationship. In other words: observing a connection between things does not automatically imply that one thing causes the other. But let's take one step at a time.

In the previous chapter, we have been engaging with **univariate data**. That means, we have only looked at one variable at a time. For instance, we were interested in the number of projects top managers have initiated and how much they differ.

If we are interested in the connection between two variables, we are dealing with **bivariate data** (Cramer and Howitt, 2004). In the following, we will be dealing with the relationship between two variables (Figure 3.1). More specifically, we will focus on the most common type of relationships, namely linear relationships.

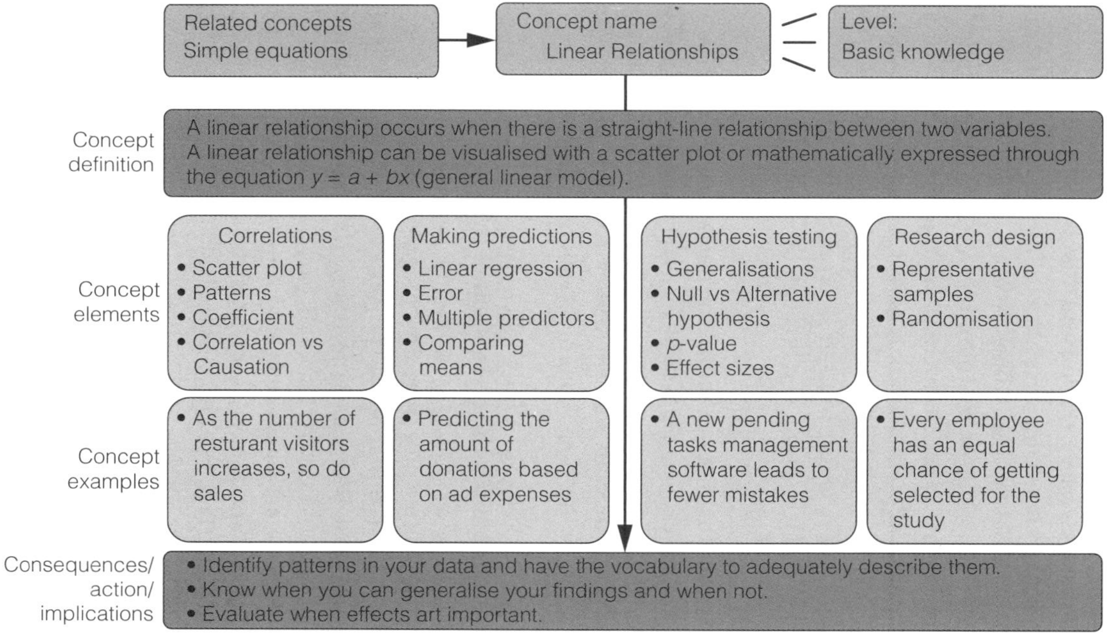
Related concepts
Simple equations
Concept name
Linear Relationships
Level:
Basic knowledge
Concept definition
A linear relationship occurs when there is a straight-line relationship between two variables.
A linear relationship can be visualised with a scatter plot or mathematically expressed through the equation y = a + bx (general linear model).
Concept elements
Correlations
• Scatter plot
• Patterns
• Coefficient
• Correlation vs Causation
Making predictions
• Linear regression
• Error
• Multiple predictors
• Comparing means
Hypothesis testing
• Generalisations
• Null vs Alternative hypothesis
• p-value
• Effect sizes
Research design
• Representative samples
• Randomisation
Concept examples
• As the number of resturant visitors increases, so do sales
• Predicting the amount of donations based on ad expenses
• A new pending tasks management software leads to fewer mistakes
• Every employee has an equal chance of getting selected for the study
Consequences/ action/ implications
• Identify patterns in your data and have the vocabulary to adequately describe them.
• Know when you can generalise your findings and when not.
• Evaluate when effects art important.

Figure 3.1 The concept of linear relationships and its components.

These are also known as straight-line relationships. The linear relationship model is also the 'working horse' of many data analysis approaches.

Figure 3.1 gives you an overview of what we are going to cover in the next few pages. Having read this chapter, you will be equipped with the knowledge necessary to thoroughly understand linear associations between things, to use your data to make *predictions*, to avoid the most common mistakes when generalising from your data and when interpreting findings. Moreover, you will learn the key terms so that you feel statistics-savvy when talking about these things. Overall, this chapter will boost your statistics confidence. So, get yourself a cup of coffee, sit down in a comfy chair and let us walk you through the miraculous world of linear relationships.

Let's start with an example. Imagine you want to know whether the number of people visiting your restaurant per day and the sales you make per day are related. Let's assume that you collected data on eight randomly selected days over a period of four months and that you wrote down your observations in Table 3.1.

The table contains all the data from your observations; however, it is quite difficult to see whether there is a pattern. To gain a better understanding of your data, you can draw a chart – a so-called **scatter plot** or **scatter diagram**. All you have to do is to draw a horizontal and a vertical axis. Usually we use the horizontal axis (the *x*-**axis**) for the variable that is considered the *predictor* and the vertical axis (the *y*-**axis**) for the variable that is considered the *outcome*. In our example, we take the number of restaurant visitors as the predictor and restaurant sales as the outcome (Figure 3.2).

With the scatter plot, a clearer picture emerges. We can see that the data are clustered around an imaginary straight line and that this

Table 3.1 Example of bivariate data.

People	2	4	6	12	14	8	10	16
Restaurant sales (in $)	200	400	500	1,200	1,500	900	1,000	1,700

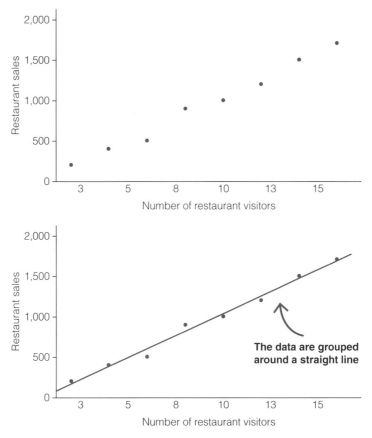

Figure 3.2 Scatter plot (top figure) and scatter plot with an imaginary straight line indicating that the data form an uphill pattern (bottom figure).

line slopes upward (Figure 3.2). The scatter plot suggests that as the number of people visiting a restaurant increases, so do the restaurant's sales. The scatter plot indicates that the number of restaurant visitors and restaurant sales are correlated.

Scatter diagrams show the correlation between two variables (Griffiths, 2009). **Correlations** are mathematical relationships between two variables. The correlation is said to be linear when the data form a more or less straight line. Let's take a look at the different types of correlations (Figure 3.3). A positive linear correlation occurs when the data show an uphill pattern. The relationship

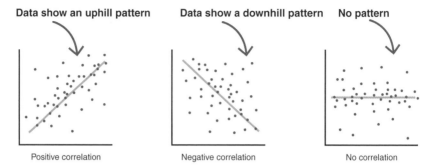

Figure 3.3 Positive linear correlation (left); negative linear correlation (middle); no correlation (right).

between the variables can be described as 'the more of X, the more of Y' or alternatively 'as X increases, so does Y'. An example would be 'the more employees, the higher the payroll costs'.

A negative linear correlation occurs when the data show a downhill pattern. The relationship between the variables can be characterised as 'the more of X, the less of Y' or 'as X increases, Y decreases'. An example would be 'the more competitors, the less market share'.

There is also the possibility that there is no correlation between two variables. This happens when the data form a random pattern (Rumsey, 2016).

So, you have just learnt what correlations are and how to correctly label different linear patterns. But why would you need that? The answer is straightforward: having the vocabulary to describe data patterns is key for building up your stats skills. You don't want to stand in front of your peers (or even worse, in front of your boss) and be at a loss for words to correctly name the grouping of your data. Saying 'the data form a linear uphill pattern' is way more elegant than saying 'the data sorta go up'.

When talking about correlations it is important to keep in mind that other types of relationships exist in addition to linear relationships (Rumsey, 2016). Figure 3.4 shows some examples of scatter plots where two variables form a relationship that is clearly non-linear. So-called inverted **U-shaped relationships** (also known as **curvilinear relationships**) occur when one variable increases as the other increases, but only up to a certain point. After that point, one of

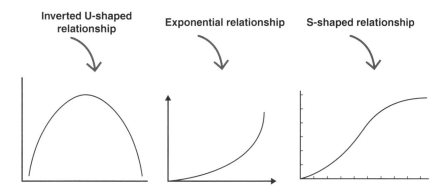

Figure 3.4 Examples of non-linear relationships: inverted U-shaped relationship (left); exponential relationship (middle); S-shaped relationship (right).

the variables continues to increase, while the other decreases. An example of an inverted U-shaped relationship would be coffee consumption and work productivity. The more coffee people drink, the higher their work productivity, but only up to a certain number of coffees. When people drink too much coffee, they might get restless and nervous, which then leads to decreased work productivity. **Exponential relationships** are another type of non-linear relationships. Exponential means that one variable is an exponent. We have seen exponential relationships in the context of contagious diseases. If someone is infected, he or she will spread the virus. And the people who have been infected will spread the virus themselves. Like this, the virus goes around and infects more and more people. Another type of non-linear relationship is an **S-shaped relationship**. There might be such a relationship between time and organisational growth. The organisational growth at first is slow, followed by a phase of rapid growth, which is then followed by a phase of consolidation in which growth slows.

It is important to understand that there are further types of relationships in addition to linear relationships. However, for the sake of keeping complexity low, non-linear patterns will not be covered in this book. The good news is that a great deal of relationships found in real life fall under the uphill–downhill linear pattern.

Visualising bivariate data in a scatter plot helps to spot whether there is a positive or a negative linear pattern. However, scatter plots do not give you 'hard facts' about the *extent* and the *nature* of this relationship. What we want is a statistic that allows us to *quantify* the direction (positive vs negative) and the strength of a linear relationship (weak vs medium vs strong). This is important as it gives us an immediate view of the relationship between two variables and thus facilitates discussions about and interpretation of that relationship. When speed and agility are of paramount importance, characterising a relationship with just one number is key.

The figure that tells us something about the direction and the strength of the linear relationship between two variables is called the **correlation coefficient**. The correlation coefficient can take values between −1 and 1 and is usually denoted by the letter 'r' (Cramer and Howitt, 2004). It is also known as the **Pearson correlation coefficient**.

But how can you draw inferences from Pearson's correlation coefficient about the direction and the strength of a linear relationship between two variables?

First of all, *the sign of the coefficient* tells you something about the direction. If Pearson's correlation coefficient is positive (positive sign), then there's a positive linear relationship. That means, the data form a linear uphill pattern. If Pearson's correlation coefficient is negative (minus sign), then there's a negative linear relationship between two variables. That means, there is a linear downhill pattern.

Second, information about the strength of the relationship is encoded in the *size of the coefficient*. The closer the coefficient is to +1 or −1, the stronger the correlation. To better understand the strength of a linear relationship, look at Figure 3.5 (strong vs weak correlation). On the left, you see a very strong positive linear relationship (Pearson correlation coefficient, $r = 0.99$). As you can see, the data do not all lie exactly on the line, but they are grouped very closely around it. In contrast, on the right, you see a weak positive linear relationship (Pearson's correlation coefficient, $r = 0.11$). Here, the data are widely scattered around the line. But what does that mean? It means that the two variables are only very loosely connected. Hence, saying that 'as X increases, Y increases' is not very accurate.

What are the threshold values for strong, medium and weak correlations you may now wonder? As often in life, there is no clear answer to this. However, there are some helpful rules of thumb for interpreting the strength of the relationship. Table 3.2 summarises these and offers you an interpretation guide for the correlation coefficient.

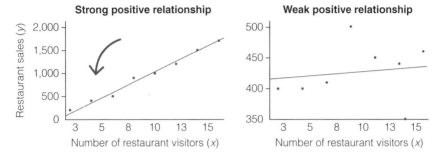

Figure 3.5 Strong correlation (left) versus weak correlation (right). The more the data form a straight line and the closer each data points lies to that line, the stronger the relationship.

Table 3.2 Interpretation guide for the correlation coefficient.

Strength of the relationship	Direction of the relationship	
	Positive	**Negative**
Perfect	+1	−1
Strong	+0.9	−0.9
Strong	+0.8	−0.8
Strong	+0.7	−0.7
Moderate	+0.6	−0.6
Moderate	+0.5	−0.5
Moderate	+0.4	−0.4
Weak	+0.3	−0.3
Weak	+0.2	−0.2
Weak	+0.1	−0.1
Zero	0	0

> ⚠ **How to say it**
>
> **Misconceptions kill the flow**
>
> Talking about correlations is often a source of confusion. This is particularly the case when the people involved in a project or a meeting have very different levels of data literacy. Some may struggle with the term 'association between variables', while others may take a 'negative relationship' as something bad or harmful. Misconceptions about statistical concepts can severely impact the discussion quality and inhibit getting into a state of flow and creativity. To avoid misunderstandings, spell out what things in your analysis really mean. Give your audience a chance to understand what you did and what its implications are.
>
> As a guideline, a good presentation or report should answer the following key questions:
>
> - What was done and what can we learn from it?
> - How was it done?
> - Why was it done?
> - Who did it?
> - When was it done?
> - (Where was it done?)

You may wonder whether you can calculate Pearson's correlation coefficient with all kinds of variables (Field, 2018). Unfortunately, you can't. Pearson's correlation coefficient requires continuous variables (interval or ratio). However, if you have two ordinal variables, you can use **Spearman's rho** or **Kendall's tau**. These statistics are versions of the correlation coefficient which are applied to ordinally ranked data (Cramer and Howitt, 2004). Remember: the values of ordinal variables are ordered, but the differences between the values are not equal. Spearman's rho and Kendall's tau can both take values between -1 and $+1$, which indicate the direction and the strength of the relationship between two ordinal variables.

If you have two categorical variables (binary or nominal), then you can use statistics such as Cramer's V (Cramer and Howitt, 2004). This statistic, however, only tells you something about the strength of the association and not about the *direction* (positive vs negative).

It may also happen that you want to investigate the relationship between a continuous variable and a binary variable (categorical variable with two categories). In this case, you should use the **biserial correlation coefficient** or the **point-biserial correlation coefficient**. The point-biserial coefficient is used when one of the variables is a true dichotomy (e.g., buy a product vs not buy a product), whereas the biserial correlation coefficient is used when one of the binary variables is an artificial dichotomy (e.g., passing vs failing an exam) (Field, 2018). Both the point-biserial and the biserial correlation coefficient range from -1 to $+1$ and thus indicate whether the relationship is positive or negative and how strong it is.

If two variables strongly correlate, does that mean that there is a cause-and-effect relationship? Can we assume that one variable causes the other? Take a deep breath. The answer is NO. Correlation only means that there is a *mathematical* relationship between two variables, but it does not mean that one causes the other, let alone that the relationship makes sense. For instance, you might be interested in the factors that increase chocolate sales and therefore collect data. Imagine you find that the number of lawyers per country and chocolate sales are positively related, so that as the number of lawyers increases, chocolate sales go up. While the statistic tells you that there is a strong connection between the number of lawyers and chocolate sales, it does not tell you whether the number of lawyers actually *leads* to an increase in chocolate sales. So, in a nutshell: don't confuse correlation with causation! Use your common sense to judge whether a correlation makes sense or not.

Understanding how predictive models work

Correlations tell you whether there's an association between two variables. However, there might be instances where you have (theoretically or empirically founded) reasons to assume that one variable *influences* the other. In such cases, you might want to make **predictions**. That means, you would use one variable to estimate changes in another variable. Simply put, predictions tell you 'how one thing influences another thing'.

With an increasing availability of data, using predictive models for decision making has rapidly gained momentum in the modern business world. Making predictions enables allocating resources more efficiently and effectively because it gives an idea of how one thing impacts another. Accordingly, predictive models are important for any kind of organisational unit ranging from marketing, to human resources management, to finance or IT. The following pages will show you how to make sound predictions and how to avoid the most common mistakes when generalising your findings beyond your data.

Suppose you came across a study that concluded that advertising expenses lead to higher fundraising effectiveness for non-profit organisations. You, as non-profit manager, therefore decide to gather data about your advertising expenses over the past 10 years and the volume of monetary donations per year. Specifically, you are interested in making predictions about the *amount of donations* you can *expect depending on the amount of money spent on the advertisement*.

To do so, you can visualise the data you collected in a scatter plot, with advertisement expenses being on the x-axis and the amount of donations on the y-axis. You then try to find the straight line through the points that fits the data as closely as possible. The line that best fits the data is known as the **line of best fit or the regression line** (Griffiths, 2008). But why would you do that? Because the line visualises how much we can expect one thing to influence the other thing. In our example, the line represents the expected amount of donations for a particular amount of advertisement expenses (Figure 3.6).

And how do you know where this line goes through? You would be ill-advised to draw it relying on your eyes and intuition. There is something better and more accurate. You can do it using the **linear regression model**. You may have heard about regression analysis before, as it is the cornerstone of analytics (and even of many AI applications). Regression analysis is just the fancy term to say: 'We use one thing to predict another thing using a linear equation'. But how does the linear equation help us find the line that is as close

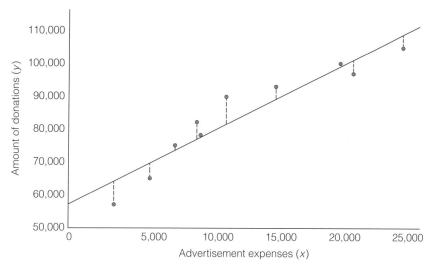

Figure 3.6 The distances between the data (the actual amount of donations) and the regression line (the estimated amount of donations) are marked with dotted lines. This is known as the error of the model or the residual. Each data point has one residual.

as possible to all data points? The way this happens is through minimising the error of the model, which is also referred to as the residual. And what's the error? It is the difference between the data that you collected (i.e., what you measured) and the prediction by your model (i.e., the regression line). Figure 3.6 illustrates what we mean by the distance between your data and the line. The bigger this difference, the worse the model is. The smaller the difference, the better the model is.

To conduct a regression analysis, we have to define a predictor variable, which in our case is the advertising expenses, and an outcome variable, which is the amount of monetary donations. The **linear regression model,** in its simplest form, is based on the equation $y = a + bx$, with a being the point where the line crosses the vertical axis (**the intercept**) and b being the **slope (or gradient)** of the line (Griffiths, 2008). Figure 3.7 visualises the components of the equation. The slope b indicates how steep the regression line is. The slope tells you how much you can expect the outcome to *change* as the predictor increases by one unit. This is visually represented in Figure 3.7 with the triangle that is attached to the regression line.

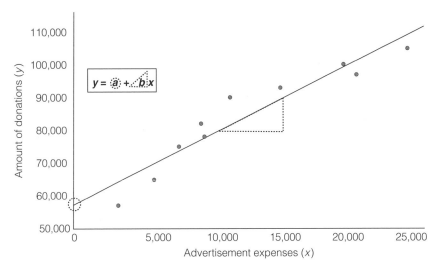

Figure 3.7 The line of best fit or regression line.

In other words, the slope is a ratio of change in the outcome (*y*) per one-unit-change in the predictor (*x*). In our example, the slope indicates how much we can expect the amount of donations to go up as the advertisement expenses increase by one dollar.

We will now elaborate a bit on the intercept and the slope to give you the necessary background to interpret these two key components of regression analysis. This will help you gain a more in-depth understanding of how predictions work. This is really key to understanding how predictive analytics work today. We acknowledge that the following pages are probably not the most enjoyable and pleasant to read. However, be ensured that we did our best to keep it as short and concise as possible. (Note that the second author's idea to include cat pictures to make these pages a bit more entertaining did not pass the editorial process.)

To find the line that best fits the data, we need to identify the values for the intercept (*a*) and the slope (*b*) that minimise the distances between the data that you have collected and the line. We will first look at the slope. The value of *b* that we are looking for can be calculated based on the following equation. No worries, we won't torture you with lengthy explanations about this equation. Just know the following: *x* is the predictor variable and *y* is the outcome variable. There are basically two things you have to do in order to fill out the equation. First, you have to calculate the differences between the mean of the advertising expenses and the actual advertisement expenses you had over recent years. Second, you have to calculate the differences between the mean of all donations and the actual amount of donations made.

Equation: Regression slope *b*

$$b = \frac{\sum_{i=1}^{n}(x_i - \bar{x})(y_i - \bar{y})}{\sum_{i=1}^{n}(x_i - \bar{x})^2}$$

where $\sum$ represents sum up, n denotes the sample size, x_i represents the *i*th value of x, y_i represents the *i*th value of y, $\bar{x}$ is the mean of x and $\bar{y}$ is the mean of y.

Anyway, let's leave this equation as it is. In our example, the slope would be 1.96. But what does this slope tell us?

To interpret the slope, we have to consider the units of the outcome variable and the predictor variable. The amount of donations and the advertisement expenses are both measured in dollars. A slope of 1.96 means that the amount of donations increases by 1.96 dollars for every 1 dollar increase in advertisement expenses.

Things become a bit more complicated when the outcome and the predictor are measured in different units. Suppose the outcome is measured as a 10-point work satisfaction scale (y) and the predictor is weeks of vacation per year (x) and you find that the slope is 1.4. What does this mean? Without considering the *units* of the outcome and the predictor variable, this number does not make much sense. Considering the units, you understand that a slope of 1.4 means an increase of 1.4 satisfaction points (change in the outcome) for every 1-week increase in vacation (change in the predictor).

And what about the intercept *a*? How do we know where the line crosses the *y*-axis? The regression equation is $y = a + bx$. The regression line represents the line of best fit and as such, the line goes through the means of the outcome and the predictor. Again here, we do not bore you with lengthy explanations about why it is like that. Just trust us. In our example, we take the amount of donations and the advertisement expenses and calculate the means for each of the variables. Moreover, we already know the value of *b* (the slope).

This allows us to figure out the value of the intercept (see equation below). The regression line crosses the y-axis at 59,890. We can interpret this value as follows: if no money is spent on advertising, our organisation is expected to receive donations of 59,890 dollars.

However, caution is warranted when interpreting the intercept. The point where our advertising expenses are zero (i.e., $x = 0$) lies outside of the range of data that we collected. Look again at Figure 3.7 and you'll see that we do not have data for advertising expenses below 2,200 dollars. As a general rule, you should never make predictions for a point that lies outside of the range of the data that you have actually collected. The relationship between the variables might change, but you don't know if it changes because you did not gather *that data*. For instance, it might be that the relationship between advertising expenses and donations is exponential and not linear for advertising expenses between 0 and 2,000 dollars. Hence, the intercept that we calculated based on *the linear model* would be a very inaccurate prediction. There are further instances where the intercept is meaningless: for example, when data near $x = 0$ do not exist (e.g., height: people cannot be 0 or 2 cm tall).

Equation: Intercept a.

$$a = \bar{y} - b\bar{x}$$
$$a = 84,200 - 1.962*12,390$$
$$a = 59,890$$

As we have seen, the linear regression model allows you to calculate the line that *best* fits your data. Cutting-edge data visualisation tools such as Tableau fortunately relieve you from calculating the line of best fit yourself. These tools compute the line of best fit and give you various statistics including the correlation coefficient. Nevertheless, in the overwhelming majority of cases, *the best fit is not the perfect fit*: it almost never occurs that all data lie exactly on the line. There is almost always a discrepancy between the data that you collected and the values that you predict. Look at Figure 3.8. The dotted lines from the actual values to the predicted values visualise this discrepancy. If we want to consider that there is an amount of error in the predictions that we make, we need to extend the regression model with an error term (Figure 3.8).

So far, we have seen how to predict an outcome from one variable. But ask yourself: are your own decisions driven by just one factor?

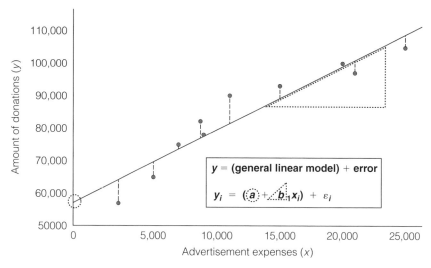

Figure 3.8 Linear regression model with error term.

Do you buy your clothes just because of the price tag? Or, do you donate money to a charity just because you are familiar with that non-profit organisation? In both cases, your answer is probably 'no'. Usually, our decisions are affected by a number of factors, with some of them exerting a stronger influence than others. Often, it therefore makes sense to consider the influence of several predictors on a given outcome. One of the compelling advantages of the linear regression model is that we can expand it and include as many predictors as we want. An additional predictor can be included as shown in the following equation:

Equation: Regression with multiple predictors

$$y = \text{(linear regression model)} + \text{error}$$

$$y_i = (a + b_1x_{1i} + b_2 x_{2i}) + \varepsilon_i$$

where y is the outcome value, a is the intercept, b_1 denotes the slope of the first predictor, b_2 is the slope of the second predictor, x_{1i} is the ith value of the first predictor variable, x_{2i} is the ith value of the second predictor variable and ε_i is the error.

As you can see, there is still an intercept a. The only difference is that we have two variables now and therefore two regression slopes (two b-values). Moreover, the visualisation of the data looks slightly different. Instead of a regression line, we now have a **regression plane**. Just as with the regression line, the regression plane seeks to minimise the distances between the data that you have collected and the values that you predict. The aim is to minimise the vertical distances between the regression plane and each data point. The length and the width of the regression plane show the b-value for the predictors (Field, 2018). It is relatively easy to visualise regressions with one or two predictors (Figure 3.9). However, with three, four, five, or even more predictors visualisations are not readily made because we cannot produce visualisations beyond three dimensions.

Let's take our example with the advertising expenses and the amount of monetary donations per year again. Imagine we also want to know whether the number of newsletters sent to our members influences the amount of donations. Hence, advertising expenses and number of newsletters would be predictors. The slope for advertising expenses is 1.51, whereas the slope for the number of newsletters is 363.17. But what does the slope for the number of newsletters mean? As we have said earlier, we have to consider the units of the predictor and the outcome to interpret the b-value. A slope of 363.17 means that the amount of donations increases by 363.17 dollars for every newsletter we send to our members.

The b-values come with a huge disadvantage: if the predictors have different units, the b-values are not directly comparable. However,

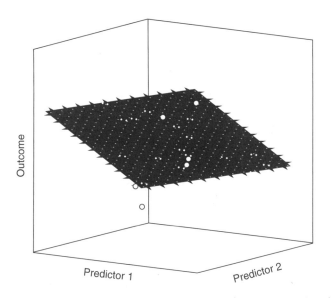

Figure 3.9 Regression with two predictors (regression plane).

there's an easy fix to that problem: we can standardise the b-values so that they can be directly compared to each other. The standardised b-values are called '**beta values**' (β). Beta values of different predictors can be easily compared to each other because they have standard deviations as their units (Field, 2018).

In our example, the standardised beta value for advertising expense is $\beta = 0.73$. This means that as advertising expenses increase by one standard deviation, donations go up by 0.73 standard deviations. The standard deviation for the amount of donation is 15,611.96 dollars, so this means donations go up by 11,369.73 dollars. Important to note is that this interpretation is true only if the influence of the number of newsletters on the amount of donations is held constant.

The standardised beta value for the number of newsletters is $\beta = 0.25$. As the number of advertisements increases by one standard deviation, donations go up by 0.25 standard deviations. This means a change of 3,902.99 dollars. Similarly, this interpretation is only true if the effect of advertising expenses on the amount of donations is held constant. Overall, the beta-values in our example suggest that advertising expenses have a comparatively stronger influence than the number of newsletters sent to our members.

Thus, one thing you can learn from this analysis is that your advertising expenses are more indicative of how much money people donate than the number of newsletters that you publish. This insight then might inform your overall marketing strategy and help you define your priorities.

 How to say it

Resisting the temptation to use jargon

Analysing and presenting data requires a lot of preparation and often a lot of expertise. The more time you invest into data and statistics, the more you become familiar with statistical terms. But beware: your audiences may not have the same level of knowledge. When throwing around words like 'correlation', 'Pearson's

▶

correlation coefficient', 'regression', 'slope' or 'intercept', you are more likely to scare off your audiences than to spark their interest for your project. Also, terms such as 'statistically significant' (see page 69) or 'large effects' (see page 76), which we will present later in this chapter, are rarely meaningful to non-statisticians. Always keep in mind that simple and clear communication is at the heart of any successful endeavour. Thus, avoid jargon (i.e., language which is meaningful to only a narrow group of people) as much as possible. Try to explain in simple terms what you mean, how you got to your conclusions, and help people interpret figures, tables, and statistics. For instance, do not anticipate that people know what a 'negative correlation coefficient of .51' means for your project. Explain what the correlation coefficient measures (i.e., strength and direction of relationship between two things; not causation) and how you would interpret it with regard to your project. If you are not sure whether you have already simplified your language appropriately, imagine how you would explain it to your parents, partner, kids or friends. You will also find a helpful overview of how to put statistical concepts in more understandable terms at the end of this chapter.

As you may have suspected already, regression analyses require continuous variables measured at the interval or ratio level. It is, however, often the case that predictors are categorical. This means, that you want to compare the differences between groups (categories!) on an outcome. Typical questions that might be of interest to you are: Do customers like our product more than the product of our competitor? Or do people volunteer longer at our organisation if we give them monetary incentives or non-monetary incentives? Such questions involve predicting an outcome based on membership in one or another group (Field, 2018). The good news is that for these kinds of questions we can again use the linear model.

Imagine that the CEO of your company entrusted you with the task to evaluate whether the company should buy ergonomic furniture for its employees. To back up your recommendation with data, you set up a small experiment. In this experiment, you measure to what extent people's health is influenced by whether their workplace is equipped with ergonomic furniture or not (Figure 3.10). Hence, the underlying question is: Does ergonomic furniture influence people's health? This question can be translated into a linear model with one binary predictor (no ergonomic furniture vs ergonomic furniture) and a continuous outcome (self-reported health status; a scale that ranges from 1 to 7). Remember, the equation for the linear model is $y = (a + bx) + \varepsilon$, where a is the intercept, b is the slope and ε is the error that we make in predicting the outcome.

x refers to the predictor variable. But what values does the predictor variable take when we compare two groups? In our example, ergonomic furniture is our binary predictor variable: employees are provided with ergonomic furniture, or not. The 'no ergonomic furniture' condition is our baseline group and in mathematical terms this means that we assign the employees in this group a 0. The ergonomic furniture condition is our experimental group and we therefore assign the employees in this group a 1. Hence, $x = 0$ means that we are referring to the no ergonomic furniture group and $x = 1$ means that we are referring to the ergonomic furniture group.

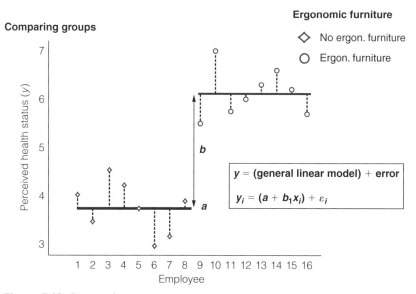

Figure 3.10 Comparing two means.

Let's look at the no ergonomic furniture group first. With the knowledge that people are in the no ergonomic furniture group, what is the best prediction we can make of their health status? It's the group mean, that is the average health status that people in the no ergonomic furniture group reported. The group mean is the best prediction because it is the summary statistic that produces the least differences between our actual data and our estimate of the outcome. In other words: the group mean comes with the least error in our predictions (Field, 2018). Basically, it is the least squared error, but never mind.

Knowing that the group mean is the best prediction of employees' health status, we also know what value to put into the equation as our estimated outcome for the no ergonomic furniture group: exactly, the group mean ($\bar{x}_{NoErgonomic} = 3.76$). The value of the predictor x is 0 because we have defined the no ergonomic furniture group as our baseline group. If we ignore the error term, the equation is shown below. As you can see, the intercept a is equal to the mean of the no ergonomic furniture group.

Equation: Intercept is equal to mean of the control group

$$y = \text{general linear model}$$

$$\text{Health Status}_i = a + b*\text{Ergonomic}_i$$

$$\bar{x}_{NoErgonomic} = a + b*0$$

$$\bar{x}_{NoErgonomic} = a$$

$$a = 3.76$$

And what about the ergonomic furniture group? Again, the best prediction we can make of people's health status in the ergonomic furniture group is the group mean. For this group, the mean is 6.13. The value of the predictor variable x is 1 because this is the value that we have assigned to the employees in the ergonomic furniture group. Keep in mind that a (the intercept) is equal to the mean of the no ergonomic furniture group ($\bar{x}_{NoErgonomic}$). If we fill out the equation and ignore the error term, we get the equation shown below. As you can see, b (the slope) represents the difference between the means of the two groups (here: $6.13 - 3.75 = 2.37$).

Equation: Calculating the slope when comparing two means

y = general linear model

Health Status$_i$ = $\boxed{a}$ + $b*$Ergonomic$_i$

$\bar{x}_{Ergonomic} = a + b*1$

$\bar{x}_{Ergonomic} = a + b$

$\bar{x}_{Ergonomic} = \bar{x}_{NoErgonomic} + b$

$b = \bar{x}_{Ergonomic} - \bar{x}_{NoErgonomic}$

$b = 6.13 - 3.76$

$b = 2.375$

> Keep in mind: the inter-
> cept $\boxed{a}$ is equal to the mean
> of the no ergonomic furni-
> ture group
>
> $a = \bar{x}_{NoErgonomic}$

Let's summarise what we have learnt so far. When we have a categorical predictor with two categories, the intercept a is equal to
the mean of the group which is defined as the control group and
the slope b represents the difference between the group means. This
difference indicates whether membership in one or another group
can be expected to influence an outcome.

You may wonder now why we have forced you to engage with all of
these equations, when in fact we could have just told you to look at
the group means and see if there's a difference. The answer is easy.
We wanted to help you develop an in-depth understanding of how
the linear model works and how you can apply it to predict whether
membership in one or another group has an impact on an outcome.

Allow us just one more remark on categorical predictors before
we move on. As we have mentioned earlier, one of the compelling
advantages of the linear regression model is that we can expand it
and include as many predictors as we want. This is also the case
when you have a categorical predictor with three or more categories. Here's an example.

Let's imagine you test the impact of three different types of humanitarian aid programmes and compare it to a control group. You
would have a group that receives material support (i.e., tools,
engines), a group that receives financial support (i.e., money), a
group that receives technical support (i.e., know-how) and a group
that does not receive any support. And let's assume you ask people
6 months after the programme has terminated to rate the quality
of their living conditions.

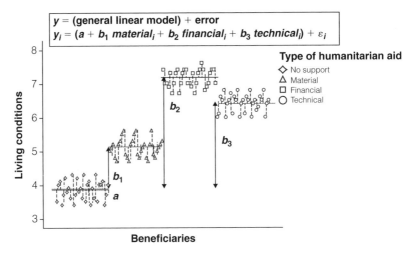

Figure 3.11 Comparing several means.

As you can see in Figure 3.11, the intercept *a* is equal to the group mean of the control group. Moreover, the *b*s (the slopes) represent the difference between the means of each group to the control group. The *b*s indicate that all types of humanitarian aid programmes help increase living conditions. The *b*-values further suggest that financial aid yielded the greatest improvements for people's living conditions compared to when no support was given.

 How to say it

Don't separate what belongs together

There is a myth that frequently pops up in data discussions: the idea that you use regression analysis when you have a continuous predictor and a continuous outcome, whereas you use something called ANOVA (analysis of variance) when you have a categorical predictor and a continuous outcome. If you attended statistics courses at school or university, you may have even learned regression analysis in one class and ANOVA in another class.

Maybe you were told that 'ANOVA is a special case of regression analysis' and that the two were 'somehow related'. Although regression analysis is used for continuous predictors and ANOVA for categorical predictors, they are the same thing. Literally. As we have shown on the previous pages, they are based on the same equation ($y = a + bx$). So, whenever you hear someone drawing a distinct line between regression analysis and ANOVA, stand up and tell them why it's an artificial difference. Be a myth buster.

By now, you have built up your statistics skills and have developed a more in-depth understanding of how to make predictions. But there is one thing which we haven't addressed yet and which often causes confusion and misconceptions – even among data scientists. Let us walk you through this point by point.

How to generalise your findings

Imagine that you work in a huge international company with several thousand employees. One of the problems that has been brought up several times at the board meetings is that employees make a lot of mistakes because they work with an old and dull pending tasks management system. Being the head of the IT department, you therefore want to introduce a new pending tasks management software that is said to be easy to handle and well structured.

Your boss does not like this idea at all (the costs for this software are very high), but after several pitches, countless emails and phone calls, he is willing to give it a shot – if you can prove that your collaboration software decreases mistakes made in the projects.

Relieved about this opportunity, you decide to use data to emphasise the utility of the new pending tasks management software. You ask 400 employees to take part in a small study in which they are asked to complete a project task – 200 employees are asked to work with the old software and the other 200 are allowed to work with the new software. Your goal is to find out whether the use of the new software influences the number of mistakes that your study participants make.

Having read our book, you know that you can use the linear model to estimate the mistakes people make. Fortunately, the results clearly indicate that the use of the new pending tasks management software has an impact, such that it radically decreases the mistakes people make (the difference between the group means is extremely large). You may therefore conclude that the new software passes the test and that it is fit to be used company-wide. But hold on, caution is warranted. What you are about to do is to generalise your findings. But is that justified? The underlying question is whether the results occurred by mere coincidence or whether you can assume that they are real. Hence, what you need to find out is whether there is sufficient evidence to assume that the results did not just happen 'by chance', 'randomly' or 'by accident' (Miller, 2017). You may insist now that the results you have obtained are obviously 'real'. You measured the number of mistakes people made and found that the use of the new software made a difference. So, why can't we necessarily assume that this difference will always occur? Because we only examined the relationship between type of software and number of mistakes among *some* of our employees. The employees who participated in your study only constitute a *subset* of all the employees in the company. Or, put more formally, what you did was to study a **sample** and not the entire **population** of interest.

A **population** is defined as the entire group of people or things which we are studying and about which we seek to make inferences (Griffiths, 2008). Populations can be defined more broadly (e.g., all human beings, all students in a country/region, all cars, or all TV commercials broadcasted within a year) or more narrowly (e.g., all donors to a non-profit organisation, all jobs ads published in a certain newspaper).

A **sample** is a (relatively small) subset of the population that you can use to make statements about the population itself (Field, 2018; Griffiths, 2008). Examples for the above-mentioned populations could be: 9,000 people from 20 different countries, 300 students of an American university, 500 cars, 3,000 print advertisements that were published over the course of a year, 200 donors to a non-profit organisation or 50 job ads published in 3 local newspapers.

In our example with the pending tasks management software, the population may include all employees of the company who work with a computer. Our sample only included a relatively small number of those employees.

What we want to know is how confident we can be that the new software really influences the number of mistakes employees make. Can we assume that the results that we found apply beyond our sample? Or did our study just produce weird random findings?

We therefore need to do something that is called **hypothesis testing**.

Hypothesis testing involves the following three steps:

1. formulate a hypothesis that you want to test;
2. examine and evaluate the evidence;
3. make a decision.

The **first step** is to make a claim about the effects we are expecting. This claim is also known as **hypothesis** (Griffiths, 2008).

Our hypothesis would be that the use of the new software influences the number of mistakes employees make. Assuming that the use of the new software has an effect, this hypothesis is called **alternative hypothesis** (and sometimes also **experimental hypothesis**). The alternative hypothesis is abbreviated with **H1**. The alternative hypothesis (H1) is tested against the **null hypothesis** (abbreviated with H0). The null hypothesis states that there is no effect. Hence, the null hypothesis would assume that the use of the new software does not influence the number of mistakes employees make. H0 is the baseline, or the default mode, against which we examine how confident we can be about our alternative hypothesis (Figure 3.12). We only reject the null hypothesis when there is sufficient evidence.

Having formulated our alternative hypothesis (H1) and the null hypothesis (H0), we now need a test to evaluate them. This is **step 2**. We assume that the null hypothesis is true (H0) and then we look at whether there is enough evidence to reject the null hypothesis and go with the alternative hypothesis (H1). To do so, we use a **test statistic**. A test statistic is a 'signal-to-noise ratio' (Field, 2018). It is a ratio between the systematic variation in the model (i.e., the

The use of the new software **does not influence** the number of mistakes employees make

The use of the new software **influences** the number of mistakes employees make

Figure 3.12 Null hypothesis (H0) versus alternative hypothesis (H1).

effect that we can explain with the fact that people either worked with the new or with the old software) and the unsystematic variation in the model (i.e., the effects we cannot explain). In other words: a test statistic tells us something about the effect relative to the error.

Equation: Test statistic

$$\text{Test statistic} = \frac{Signal}{Noise} = \frac{Systematic\ variation}{Unsystematic\ variation}$$

Look at Figure 3.13. We can explain the differences between the group means with the fact that employees worked with different software. This is the systematic variation. What we can't explain, however, is the difference between each employee and the respective group mean. For instance, why did some employees in the 'old software group' make ten mistakes, while others made eight mistakes? We simply don't know.

Generally, we can say that we want large test statistics. This means that the signal is bigger than the noise: the systematic variation (i.e., everything we can explain) is bigger than the unsystematic variation (i.e., everything we cannot explain). For instance, a signal-to-noise ratio greater than 1 means that there is more variation that we can explain than we can't explain.

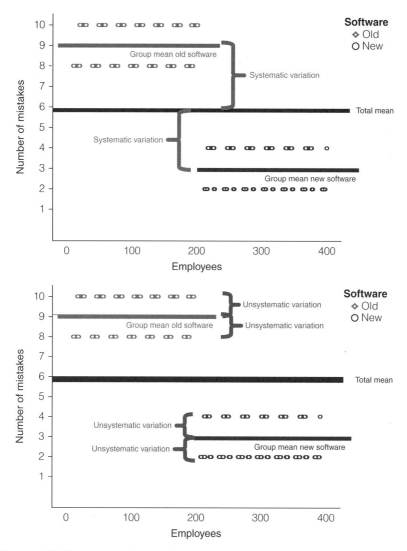

Figure 3.13 Signal-to-noise ratio: systematic variation versus unsystematic variation.

There are a lot of different approaches to calculate test statistics (e.g., t, χ^2, F). Each of these approaches is based on a distribution that tells us how probable it is that we would get a signal-to-noise ratio of at least that size, assuming that the differences between the treatments occur by mere chance (i.e., assuming that the null hypothesis is true and there is no real effect). The probability of obtaining a certain signal-to-noise ratio under the assumption of the null hypothesis is known as the **p-value**. It is expressed as a number between 0 and 1. The lower the p-value, the more unlikely is it that we would get such a big effect size and could explain so much variance in the data, if the differences occurred by mere chance. There is an inverse relationship between the size of test statistics and the p-value: as the test statistic gets bigger, the p-value gets smaller. The more variation we can explain in the data (expressed by a large test statistic), the less evidence there is to assume that the differences occurred by mere chance (expressed by a small p-value).

In our software study, we get a very big signal-to-noise ratio. It means that the number of mistakes our employees make can be mainly explained by whether they use the old or the new software. This is also reflected in a very small p-value of .001. What does this p-value mean? Assuming that the use of the old or new software does not influence the number of mistakes our employees make (i.e., the null hypothesis is true), there is a 0.1% chance that we would obtain a signal-to-noise ratio at least as big as the one we have.

As this is highly unlikely to happen, the p-value indicates strong evidence against the null hypothesis. We therefore reject the null hypothesis (i.e., type of software has no effect on the number of mistakes).

Still a bit confused? No worries, Figure 3.14 illustrates the inverse relationship between the size of test statistics and the p-value.

And what is the threshold for rejecting the null hypothesis? When do we have sufficient evidence for the alternative hypothesis? This is what we address with **step 3** (make a decision). You need to set a predetermined cut-off point for how small the p-value must be at least so that you reject the null hypothesis (Figure 3.15). This cut-off point is also known as the **significance level (or alpha level)**. The significance level determines how confident we must be that an effect did not happen by mere coincidence. It is a widely held convention across disciplines to choose an alpha level of 0.05. This means that we accept a 5% risk of deciding that an effect exists when in fact it does not exist. If we get a p-value that is equal or less than the alpha level, then we found strong support for the alternative hypothesis and reject the null

Test statistic	p-value	What does the p-value tell us?
↑ Test statistic = $\dfrac{\textbf{Signal}}{\text{Noise}}$	p-value ↓	**It is unlikely** that we would get a test statistic of at least this size, assuming that the differences occur by mere chance (H0) → indication that there is a real effect (H1)
↓ Test statistic = $\dfrac{\text{Signal}}{\textbf{Noise}}$	*p*-value ↑	**It is likely** that we would get a test statistic of at least this size, assuming that the differences occur by mere chance (H0) → indication that there is no real effect (H0)

Figure 3.14 Inverse relationship between the size of test statistics and the p-value.

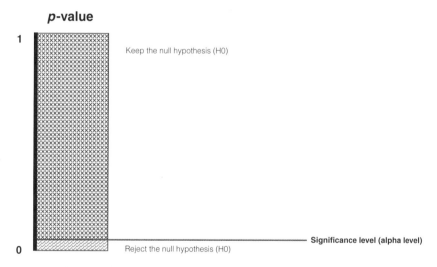

Figure 3.15 Significance level and its implications.

hypothesis. If the p-value is greater than the alpha level, then we fail to reject the null hypothesis (Field, 2018).

So, in our example we have concluded that the people who use the new software differ 'significantly' in terms of the number of mistakes they make. But keep in mind that although there is strong evidence that the type of software influences the number of mistakes, we can never be absolutely sure. There is no guarantee because we go with the alternative hypotheses based on *how likely* it is that we are making a mistake when rejecting the null hypotheses. Although it might be very unlikely that we make a mistake, there always remains a small probability that we are wrong.

The difference between significant and important effects

There is a common fallacy that is often made; that is, to confuse *significant* effects (i.e., non-random effects) with *important* effects (i.e., meaningful effects). 'Significant' only means that we found enough evidence in our data to conclude that an effect might be real. However, the question is whether this effect is also meaningful. When talking about meaningful effects, we are referring to effect *sizes*. Effect sizes provide (absolute and standardised) measures of the magnitude of an effect (Field, 2018).

Effect sizes either capture the sizes of differences between groups or the sizes of relationships between continuous variables. The most commonly used measures of effect sizes are: **Cohen's *d*** (comparison between two group means), **eta squared** (proportion of variation in an outcome that is associated with membership in different groups), the **odds ratio** (odds of an event occurring in one group compared to another group) and **Pearson's correlation coefficient** (strength and direction of the relationship between two continuous variables) (Field 2018). You don't need to know how they are calculated. What is important is that you know that effect sizes capture the magnitude of an effect. Note that Pearson's correlation coefficient is also used as a measure of effect size because it expresses the size of the relationship between two variables. Remember that Pearson's correlation coefficient indicates the strength and the direction of an association but does not discriminate between predictor and outcome variables (see page 21). That means, strictly speaking, it does not tell you whether one thing caused the other. However, the correlation coefficient is often used in a way that suggests that it reflects aspects of cause and effect.

Let's illustrate the difference between p-*values* and *effect sizes* with an example. Imagine you were the CEO of a chocolate factory and you wanted to evaluate whether you should substitute chocolate bar B with chocolate bar A. Based on the experimental study that your team conducted, you find that participants liked chocolate bar A significantly more than chocolate bar B. The *p*-value is below the traditional 0.05 criterion, indicating that you can be very confident to assume that the difference did not occur by chance. The *p*-value tells you how confident you can be to assume that customers – beyond your study – like chocolate bar A more than chocolate bar B. What the *p*-value doesn't indicate, however, is how big this effect is. This is where effect sizes come into play. By using a measure of effect size, you can conclude whether chocolate bar A is preferred only a little, moderately, or very much over chocolate bar B. And why would you want to know this? Because the *p*-value answers the question 'is there a real difference?', whereas effect sizes tell you 'how big is this difference?'. If the difference between the chocolate bars is marginally small, you might want to reconsider whether it is really worth substituting one chocolate bar with the other – although the effect was significant.

Data conversation (continued)

Elaine was shocked. The results from a survey among more than 4,000 participants suggested that participants liked the competitor's drink significantly more than the energy drink from Elaine's company. Barbara, her co-worker, looked over the results that Elaine had just printed out and said: 'Well, yes, the significant results indicate that customers prefer the other energy drink over our drink. But that might not be the entire story. What about the *magnitude* of this effect?'. Elaine had heard about effect sizes; however, she had not calculated it. She quickly consulted her statistics book and figured that eta squared was an adequate measure of effect size for her data. She obtained an eta squared of .01, which is a very small and negligible effect. 'So, how should we interpret the findings in the light of the small effect size?', Elaine asked. 'First of all, this very small effect size is reassuring as it implies that the difference between the two energy drinks is not really meaningful', Barbara explained. She also pointed to an important aspect about *p*-values that Elaine hadn't known. The *p*-values are linked with the sample size. The sample size

▶

77

influences whether differences are significant or not. *In large samples, even very small and negligible effects can be significant.* In small samples, however, even very big effects can be non-significant. Barbara added that the large sample (i.e., 4,000 participants) in the survey rendered even the very small difference in the liking of the two energy drinks significant. 'Thanks a lot, Barbara', Elaine said. Although the results from the study were not as Elaine had wished, she now could look at them in a more nuanced way. Considering not just the *p*-values but also effect sizes helped her gain a richer picture and not fall into alarmism.

By now, you have learned how to draw inferences from your data and distinguish statistically significant from practically meaningful results. However, there is one important aspect upon which we haven't touched yet: that is, how to make sure that your conclusions are valid in the light of the data you collected. This is a matter of research design. Research design refers to the plan that you set up to answer your research question (e.g., do customers like chocolate bar A or B better?). Not having a sound research design can come at high costs because it may very quickly contaminate and invalidate the conclusions you draw from your data.

There are two key aspects which you need to consider to render your study worthwhile.

1. **About whom do you aim to make inferences? And is your sample representative of the wider group to which you seek to generalise your findings?**

   Your sample is representative when it (more or less) reflects the key characteristics of the population of interest. Common examples of such key characteristics include gender, age, education, socioeconomic status, marital status, job position or consumer behaviour. Failure to account for sample representativeness is detrimental as it leads to the findings of your analysis being wrongly attributed. For instance, imagine that you wanted to generalise your findings to all employees in your company, but had only included managers from the middle management. Strictly speaking, your sampling approach does not allow you to draw inferences beyond managers from middle management. But how do you ensure sample representativeness? By using probability sampling methods. Probability methods use random selection, which means that subjects (e.g., people) are randomly selected from the population of interest and that each subject has an equal chance of getting selected. Let's take the software example again. Random selection means that every employee would have the same chance to participate in the study. However, it is not always possible to use a probability sampling method because it would take too much time or may be too expensive or because you do not have a comprehensive list of all subjects of your population. Note that if every subject should have an equal chance of getting selected, you have to know in advance who belongs to your population of interest. We can think of a lot of instances where this is not given or very difficult to find out (e.g., when your population of interest is single parents in Europe or car owners in South America). Thus, the other option is to use non-probability sampling methods. This refers to sampling approaches in which not every subject has the same chance of being selected. Common non-probability sampling methods include convenience sampling (i.e., you select subjects who happen to be most accessible such as students or members of your non-profit organisations), voluntary response sampling (i.e., people volunteer themselves to participate in your study, for instance by responding to a consumer response survey) or snowball sampling (i.e., you recruit people for your study via other people). Non-probability sampling methods are often easier, cheaper and more feasible, but also come with decreased representativeness. The generalisations you can make about the population of interest are weaker (or more questionable) and your inferences may be more limited. Nevertheless, you should still try to make it as representative of the population as possible.

A common misconception about representativeness is that it means the *number of subjects in your sample*. We sometimes hear analysts or consultants talking about *representative samples*, while meaning *large samples*. Beware that just because 100 or 500 people participated in a study, does not necessarily mean that the sample is representative of the wider group to which the inferences should be drawn. Thus, always ask for clarification when someone speaks about 'representative samples'.

2. Are there any aspects that might distort or confound your inferences?

The examples that we have used to explain hypothesis testing (i.e., the software study and the chocolate bar study) were both based on an experimental research design. The purpose of experimental research designs is to establish cause-and-effect relationships. In the software example, for instance, we wanted to find out whether the use of an old software or a new software influences the number of mistakes our employees make. In experimental studies, there are at least two groups that are compared in terms of an outcome (e.g., number of mistakes the employees make). In the simplest case, one group receives a treatment (experimental group), while the other group does not receive the treatment (control group). Sometimes you have no control group but several experimental groups (e.g., one group eats chocolate bar A and the other group eats chocolate bar B). As popular as experimental research has become in business contexts, as much caution is warranted when conducting such studies. There are several aspects that might invalidate your findings.

One of the most fundamental aspects refers to the way that the participants in your sample are assigned to the groups. In a true experiment, people are randomly assigned to the treatments. This is the case, for instance, if the 400 people participating in your software study were randomly assigned to either the old-software group or the new-software group. However, if you decided yourself who is in the old-software group and who is in the new-software group or if you put entire teams in either group, then it would be a quasi-experimental design. Quasi-experimental designs have a considerable disadvantage compared to genuine experimental designs. The lack of random assignment potentially leads to systematic differences between the groups. Let's imagine that you conducted the software study and asked people from the marketing department to work with the old software and people from the IT department to work with the new software. Assume now that your findings would show significant and meaningful differences in the number of mistakes people make working with each software. The problem is that you cannot rule out the possibility that these differences are due to the pre-existing IT skills instead of the software itself.

There are a number of further aspects that may result in systematic differences between the groups in quasi-experimental research (e.g., selection-history threat, which means that the treatment groups are differently influenced by extraneous or historical events).

Whenever there are things that confuse the relationship between the independent variable (e.g., software) and the dependent variable (e.g., number of mistakes), we are dealing with confounding variables. Confounding variables, also referred to as confounders, are things that correlate with both the dependent variable and the independent variable. Take the above-mentioned example with the people from the marketing and IT department. It is possible that participants in the new-software group have better IT skills than the participants in the old-software group and that people with greater IT skills generally make less mistakes using software. IT skills might be a confounding variable (Figure 3.16). The results seem to show that the new software decreases the number of mistakes, which may not be true. Confounding variables lead to a mixing or distortion of effects so that the results do not reflect the actual relationship between the independent and dependent variable. The trouble with confounding factors is, however, that they are not always obvious or known. Random assignment is a common strategy used to control confounding variables as it allows the confounding variables to have their effects across the sample. Thus, whenever possible use true experimental designs instead of quasi-experimental designs.

Using randomisation is a way to minimise the impact of confounding variables *before* data collection. However, if you have already gathered data (and used quasi-experimental or survey designs),

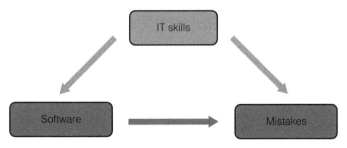

Figure 3.16 Example of a confounding variable.

you can use statistical methods to control for potential confounders. The linear model assists you with this. Specifically, it tests whether a predictor has an effect on an outcome after removing the variance for which the confounding variable accounts. This allows you to see the 'clean effect' of the predictor on the outcome.

Overall, how can you evaluate whether your conclusions are valid in the light of the data you collected? First, ask yourself (or your analyst) to what extent your sample allows you to make inferences to the population of interest. Second, think about potential confounders and to what extent you managed to control for their influence.

Key take-aways

Sometimes we all want more: more money, more power or more happiness. Also, when analysing data, we sometimes strive for more, namely generalisable insights. It is helpful to describe the data that we have collected. But often, we want to go beyond our data and extrapolate from them. For instance, we might want to make statements about all our volunteers, not just about those who participated in our survey. Or, we might want to generalise the patterns in the consumption behaviour of the millennials in our study to all millennials in our country. Going beyond our data means that we can make generalisable statements. If we can infer under which conditions volunteers stay the longest in our organisation, we can adjust our volunteer management accordingly. Or, if we can infer what products millennials prefer, we can promote these products more intensively (Field, 2018). But getting from your data to generalisations can be a tricky endeavour. The following questions should help you with this.

1. Look at the scatter plot. Do your data form a linear uphill or downhill pattern? If this is the case, calculate the correlation between your variables. If you find a linear correlation between your variables, you can use the general linear model to make predictions (i.e., use one variable to predict the other).

2. Check the measurement level of the variables. Is the outcome variable continuous? Is the predictor continuous (➤if the outcome and the predictor variables are continuous, use regression; if the outcome variable is continuous but the predictor variable is categorical, compare means)?

3. What is your (alternative) hypothesis? What is the corresponding null hypothesis? What cut-off point do you define to reject the null hypothesis (significance level)?

4. Is there a significant effect? And if so, is it also meaningful?

5. Is the sample representative of the wider group (population) to which you aim to generalise your findings?

6. Did you account for potential confounding factors via research design (e.g., true experiments that use random group assignment) or via statistical methods?

 Traps

Analytics traps

- Confusing correlation (i.e., mathematical relationship between two variables: 'as X increases, so does Y' or 'as X increases, Y decreases') with causation (i.e., one thing causes the other).

- Not looking at the scatter plot and classifying the relationship between two variables as linear when in fact it is curvilinear or exponential.

- Choosing an inappropriate correlation coefficient that does not fit the measurement level of your variables (e.g., calculate Spearman's rho when you should use Cramer's V).

- Making predictions outside of the range of observed values (e.g., predicting the amount of donation based on ad expenses that lie outside of the range of data that you collected).

- Interpreting the intercept although it does not make sense (e.g., because there are no data near $x = 0$ such as for height: people cannot be 0 or 2 cm tall).

- Comparing b-values instead of beta-values when using several predictors in a regression model.

- Generalising findings from a sample (e.g., a random sample of members of a non-profit organisation) to a population (e.g., all members of that non-profit organisation) without doing hypothesis testing and checking whether the effects occurred by mere coincidence or whether they are real.

- Generalising findings from a non-representative sample to the population of interest.

- Not knowing your sample or the way that the data was collected.
- Not controlling for the influence of confounding variables.

Communication traps

- Ignoring people's level of data literacy and assuming that everyone knows the same things as you do.
- Using jargon to demonstrate your data literacy.
- Failing to explain the key aspects of your analysis and the resulting implication (what was done and what can we learn from it? How was it done? Why was it done? Who did it? When was it done? Where was it done?).
- Talking of regression analysis (continuous predictor and a continuous outcome) and ANOVA (analysis of variance; categorical predictor and a continuous outcome) as if they were two different pairs of shoes. Regression analysis and ANOVA are the same thing because they are based on the same equation ($y = a + bx$).
- Speaking of significant effects (i.e., non-random effects) when you mean important effects (i.e., meaningful effects) and vice versa.
- Speaking of representative samples when you mean large samples.
- Using jargon instead of plain language when talking about statistics (see Table 3.3).

Table 3.3 Dos and don'ts when talking about statistics.

Don't Jargon	Do Plain language
Univariate data vs bivariate data	You look at one thing vs You look at the connection between two things.
Correlation	A mathematical relationship between things.
Positive linear correlation	The data show an uphill pattern. The relationship between two things can be described as 'the more of X, the more of Y' or alternatively 'as X increases, so does Y'.

Don't Jargon	Do Plain language
Negative linear correlation	The data show a downhill pattern. The relationship between two things can be characterised as 'the more of X, the less of Y' or 'as X increases, Y decreases'.
Direction of the correlation coefficient	Tells you whether the data form an uphill or downhill pattern. This is indicated by the sign of the coefficient (positive or negative sign).
Strength of the correlation coefficient	Tells you how strongly or loosely connected things are. This is indicated by the size of the coefficient. The closer it is to $+1$ or -1, the stronger the connection.
Making predictions	You use one thing to estimate changes in another thing. Simply put, predictions help you understand 'how one thing influences another thing'.
Regression analysis	You use a linear equation to see how one thing influences another thing.
Regression line/line of best fit	The line that fits the data as closely as possible.
The slope (b)	Indicates how steep the regression line is. The slope tells you how much you can expect the outcome to *change* as the predictor increases by one unit.
The intercept (a)	Indicates where the regression line crosses the y-axis. This tells you the amount of an outcome when the predictor is zero (e.g., what amount of donations we expect to receive if we spend no money on advertising).
Error	The difference between the data you collected and the values that you estimate (or predict).
Population	The entire group of people or things about which you seek to make inferences (e.g., car drivers in a country; employees under 40 in American companies).

▶

Don't Jargon	Do Plain language
Sample	A (relatively small) subset of the entire group of people or things in which you are interested.
Alternative hypothesis (H1)	Makes the claim that there is an effect.
Null hypothesis (H0)	Makes the claim that there is no effect.
p-value	Indicates how likely it is to assume that the results occurred by mere chance.
Significance level (alpha level)	Determines how confident we must be that an effect did not happen by mere coincidence. It is a widely held convention across disciplines to choose an alpha level of 0.05. This means that we accept a 5% risk of deciding that an effect exists when in fact it does not exist.
Effect sizes	Provide measures of the importance of an effect. Such measures tell you how big or meaningful an effect is.
Representative sample	A sample is representative when it reflects the key characteristics of the wider group of interest.
Random sampling	People (or things) are randomly selected from the wider group of interest and each one has the same chance to participate in the study.
Random assignment/ Randomisation	Random assignment is a key feature of 'true experiments'. It means that the study participants (i.e., those who are in the sample) are randomly assigned to the treatment groups.
Confounding variable	Things that confuse the relationship between two other things (e.g., software and number of mistakes).

Further resources

For an online tool that creates scatter plots for bivariate data:

https://mathcracker.com/scatter_plot

For an informative and accessible text on the concept of statistical significance:

https://hbr.org/2016/02/a-refresher-on-statistical-significance

For an entertaining video on the difference between statistically significant versus meaningful effects:

https://www.youtube.com/watch?v=oGgsKmi_lyA

Chapter

Understanding complex relationships: Asking for the when and why

What you'll learn

We are living in an increasingly complex and multifaceted world. In order to successfully navigate modern business challenges, we therefore need to understand and adequately capture complex relationships. This chapter discusses complex relationships where one thing influences the relationship between two other things (moderation) or where the relationship between two things is explained by another thing (mediation). We will illustrate with practical examples why managers and experts profit from knowledge of moderation and mediation analysis.

Data conversation

It was Kenny's and James' first opportunity to prove their communication expertise to their colleagues. Ten months ago, Kenny and James joined the non-profit organisation as trainees and ever since they had been passionate about their job. It didn't take long until the Head of Communication entrusted them with the task to develop a communication concept for the website of the organisation. To do so, Kenny and James conducted an extensive literature research which led them to the conclusion that visual images play a crucial role in online communication. Previous studies consistently indicated that emotional images (i.e., images showing

▶

---

either happy or sad people) attract users' attention and increase their engagement with the web content.

'But does it matter whether we use happy or sad images?', Kenny asked his colleague. The question turned into a lengthy discussion that resulted in no clear answer. However, both were curious to find out whether happy or sad images were more effective in retaining users on the website. They therefore set up two versions of the website, one with only happy images and the other with only sad images. They then invited 80 people to visit the website and randomly assigned them to either the happy image version or the sad image version. All participants had to fill out a questionnaire. The subsequent analysis suggested that the type of imagery did not have a substantial impact on the length of the website visit (Figure 4.1). 'The findings indicate that we can use both happy and sad images on our website', Kenny figured. But by chance, he remembered that the questionnaire also captured whether the participants were members of the non-profit organisation or not. Did their membership status possibly influence whether they were more responsive to sad or happy images?

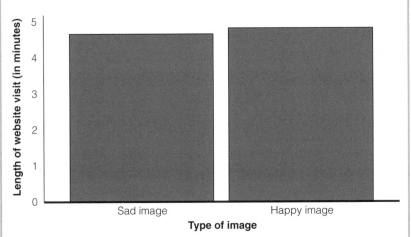

Figure 4.1 Effect of type of imagery (sad vs happy) on the length of users' website visit.

Often it is the simple things in life that make us happy: going for a walk, enjoying a colourful sunset or spending time with our loved ones. But as pleasant as these simple things can be, the world is often quite complicated. A lot of things are contingent upon each other. For instance, the extent to which we become more generous with age may depend on our socioeconomic status. And sometimes the effect of one thing is explained by another thing: we may feel happier, the better feedback we get. This may be due to the fact that good feedback increases our self-esteem, which then translates into more happiness.

Fortunately, statistics allow us to examine these kinds of complex relationships (Field, 2018). Whenever we want to find out to what extent one thing (e.g., socioeconomic status) influences the relationship between two other things (e.g., age and generosity), we use **moderation analysis**. Whenever we aim to understand to what extent the relationship between two things (e.g., feedback and happiness) is explained by another thing (e.g., self-esteem), we use **mediation analysis**. Put in more analytical terms, moderation and mediation both enable us to better understand the relationship between a predictor and an outcome by testing how a third variable fits into this relationship (Figure 4.2).

When we conduct a **moderation** analysis (Figure 4.3), we are interested in something that is called an **interaction effect** (Field, 2018). We want to find out to what extent a variable affects the *strength or direction* of the relationship between a predictor and an outcome variable (Fritz and Arthur, 2017). Engaging with moderator variables is crucial for several reasons. First, it allows for a more nuanced understanding of the world. Moderation analysis is a data-based way to say 'it depends'. Second, some effects are 'hidden' in that they only show when you consider the influence of a moderator variable. Without taking into account the moderator variable, you may wrongfully conclude that there is no effect. This can have a detrimental impact on the quality and robustness of your decisions.

Let's illustrate this with an example (Figure 4.4). Suppose that we collect data to better understand the relationship between people's involvement in humanitarian issues (such as fighting famine in Africa) and the amount of donations that they make. We analyse this data and state that there is a positive relationship between involvement and the amount of donation: the more people are

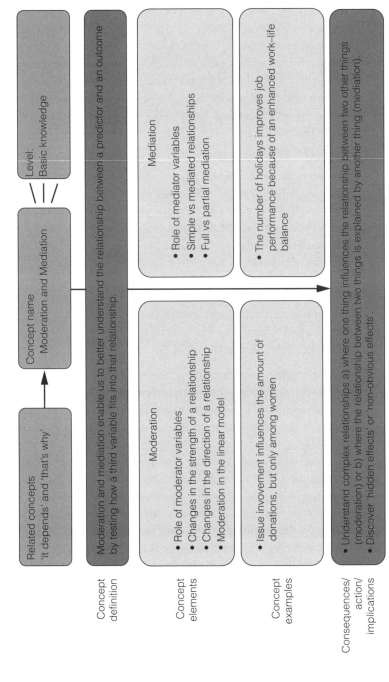

Figure 4.2 The concepts of moderation and mediation and their components.

Related concepts
'it depends' and 'that's why'

Concept name
Moderation and Mediation

Level:
Basic knowledge

Concept definition

Moderation and mediation enable us to better understand the relationship between a predictor and an outcome by testing how a third variable fits into that relationship.

Concept elements

Moderation

• Role of moderator variables
• Changes in the strength of a relationship
• Changes in the direction of a relationship
• Moderation in the linear model

Mediation

• Role of mediator variables
• Simple vs mediated relationships
• Full vs partial mediation

Concept examples

• Issue involvement influences the amount of donations, but only among women

• The number of holidays improves job performance because of an enhanced work–life balance

Consequences/ action/ implications

• Understand complex relationships a) where one thing influences the relationship between two other things (moderation) or b) where the relationship between two things is explained by another thing (mediation).
• Discover 'hidden effects' or 'non-obvious effects'.

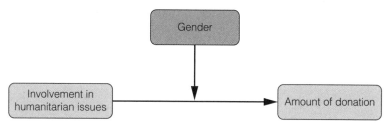

Figure 4.3 Moderated relationship (conceptual moderation model).

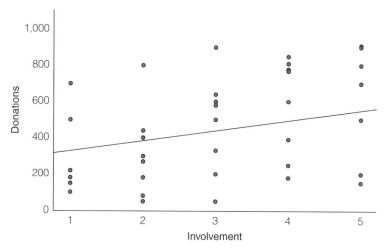

Figure 4.4 Relationship between involvement and amount of donations.

involved in humanitarian issues (say have friends or family members in an affected region), the more they donate. Moreover, the relationship does not seem to be that strong (the line is rather flat).

Assume that we had also collected data on people's gender and that we can therefore classify them as female or male. Doing the same analysis but with gender as a (categorical) moderator variable, we would see that the relationship between involvement and amount of donation varies depending on whether people identify as male or female (Figure 4.5). There is no relationship between involvement and the amount of donation for men (because the line is almost completely flat in our fictitious example), whereas for women, there is a strong positive relationship. As women's involvement increases, so does the amount of donations that they make (as the dotted line is quite steep).

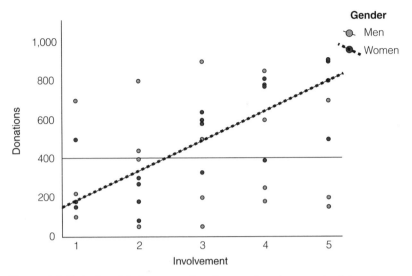

Figure 4.5 Relationship between involvement and amount of donations among women and men (i.e., gender = moderator variable).

This is an example for a moderator variable that influences the *strength* of the relationship between a predictor and an outcome. In the dialogue box (below) you see what it means if a moderator variable changes the *direction* of the relationship between a predictor and an outcome.

Data conversation (continued)

An interesting pattern emerged from Kenny's and James' experiment. The findings suggested that people's membership status (member vs non-member) influenced whether they were more responsive to sad or happy images. The data showed that *members* spent significantly more time on the website when they were assigned to the website version with only sad images. In contrast, non-members remained significantly longer on the website when they were directed to the version with only happy images (Figure 4.6). 'This is interesting and might have practical implications', James said. The results suggest that we might want to use sad images for subpages that primarily address our members and happy images for subpages that are directed at a general public.

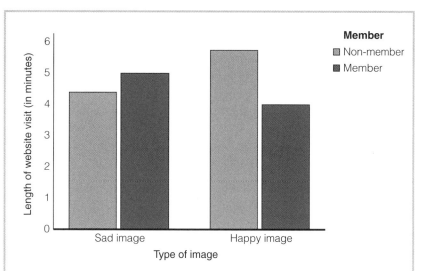

Figure 4.6 Effect of type of imagery (sad vs happy) and membership status (non-member vs member) on the length of users' website visit.

Although they had to validate the findings with more data, taking into account the potential influence of membership status – a moderating variable – helped Kenny and James to develop a more sophisticated communication approach. At the end of the day, both felt tired but satisfied. They were looking forward to presenting their communication strategy to the Head of Communication the next day.

The examples provided illustrate different ways of how a third variable can influence the relationship between two other variables. In the donation example, it has been shown that gender (moderator) influences the strength of the relationship between involvement and donation, such that there is an effect for women but not for men. In the website example, however, membership status (moderator) has flipped the entire interpretation, such that the positive effect of sad images for members is completely reversed for non-members.

But how does moderation analysis fit into the general linear model? As we have seen previously, we can add predictors to the linear model. To test for moderation, we add both predictors and then add a third term that includes the interaction of the two predictors.

The interaction can be calculated by multiplying the two predictors. The model then reads as follows:

Equation: Moderation

$$y_i = (a + b_1x_{1i} + b_2x_{2i} + b_3x_{1i}{}^*x_{2i}) + \varepsilon_i$$

where y is the outcome value, a denotes the intercept, b_1 is the slope of the first predictor, b_2 is the slope of the second predictor, x_{1i} is the ith value of the first predictor variable, x_{2i} is the ith value of the second predictor variable and ε_i is the error.

In contrast, **mediation** occurs when the relationship between a predictor and outcome can be explained by a third variable – a **mediator** (Field, 2018). A mediator provides an explanation for why the relationship between a predictor and an outcome exists. Mediation analyses basically enable you to say 'here's why'. Such analyses are important because they help to uncover the processes and mechanisms by which a predictor influences an outcome (Agler and De Boeck, 2017; Rucker *et al.*, 2011). This way, mediation analyses allow you to understand the behaviours and attitudes of your employees, customers or political allies on a more profound level. The better you understand your stakeholders, the better you can adjust to their needs and the more successful you are in gaining their support.

The following example should clarify the concept of mediation. Imagine that your HR team had discovered that the number of holidays taken by your staff was positively related to their job performance. The more holidays your employees have, the better their job performance (Figure 4.7). You may, of course, wonder why this positive relationship exists. The number of holidays presumably has a positive impact on job performance because employees perceive their work–life-balance to be very good. Figure 4.8 shows the respective mediation model. The model suggests that the relationship between holidays and job performance operates through an increase in the perceived work–life balance.

Figure 4.7 Simple relationship between a predictor and an outcome.

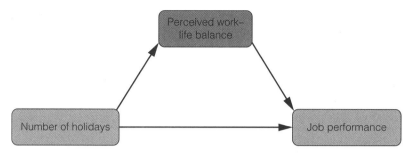

Figure 4.8 Mediated relationship (conceptual mediation model).

But how can we determine if a variable explains – that is, mediates – the relationship between two other variables? According to Baron and Kenny (1986), mediation can be identified based on a three-step approach. First, the starting point consists of testing for a significant relationship between the predictor and the outcome variable (e.g., number of holidays and job performance). Second, there must be a significant relationship between the predictor and the mediator variable. That means that the number of holidays must significantly influence people's perceived work–life balance. And third, there must be a significant relationship between the mediator and the outcome variable (i.e., perceived work–life balance has to significantly predict job performance).

We speak of *full mediation* (or, complete mediation) when the predictor no longer shows a significant relationship with the outcome variable after the mediator variable has been entered into the analysis. In our example, this would imply that perceived work–life balance fully explains the effect of the number of holidays on job performance.

Partial mediation occurs when the predictor's effect on the outcome is reduced but is still significant after the mediator variable has been added. The occurrence of partial mediation can be viewed as an indication that there might be further mediator variables. In our example, partial mediation would imply that perceived work–life balance is not the only mechanism explaining the relationship between the number of holidays and job performance and that we might want to include additional mediator variables in our analysis (e.g., we might have reason to assume that the relationship between number of holidays and job performance is also explained by happiness such that the more holidays people have, the happier they are and, as a result, the better they work).

⚠ **How to say it**

Keep it short and simple – but not at the expense of clarity

We often find ourselves in situations where we have to simplify and leave out details. This may be because we are given time constraints for our presentations or space constraints for written reports. Such constraints can be helpful as they force you to focus on the things that really matter. Nonetheless, they may also seduce you to remove visualisations that are vital to a thorough understanding of your data analysis or your findings. You may think that certain charts take too much time to be explained or too much space in your report and that it is better to drop them. But be careful about removing visualisations – especially when presenting complex relationships. Moderation and mediation are abstract terms and without proper explanation your audience might easily get lost. If this happens, you will have a hard time maintaining their attention, let alone getting across your message. To avoid confusion and disinterest, it is often very helpful to present the conceptual model underlying your moderation and mediation analysis. Conceptual models offer an at-a-glance summary of the variables that you included in your analysis and visualise how they relate to each other. That means, conceptual models give your audience an immediate overview of what is the predictor, the moderator/mediator and the outcome. You can find examples of conceptual models in Figure 4.3 (Conceptual moderation model) and Figure 4.8 (Conceptual mediation model).

Moreover, if you intend to remove a visualisation, ask yourself: What is the value added of this visualisation? To what extent does this visualisation help my audience understand the relationship that I have investigated? Or to what extent does it enhance people's understanding of my findings? What would happen if I omitted this visualisation? Could I have the same effect by just using words?

If you see that words cannot substitute the benefit of a visualisation, then keep it. You may also want to ask two of your colleagues (with similar levels of data literacy) for feedback: one of them receives the version with the diagram and the other receives the version with plain text. Ask them about their understanding of your analysis and check whether the inclusion of the visualisation led to greater comprehension and memorability of your findings.

Key take-aways

Successfully navigating the complex world we live in requires that we understand under which conditions certain effects occur (moderation) and what the key mechanisms driving these effects (mediation) are. Concepts of moderation and mediation are thus a 'must know' for anyone involved with data analysis. You may find the following questions helpful when dealing with moderation or mediation analysis.

1. Do you have reason to assume that the strength or direction of a relationship between a predictor and an outcome is influenced by a third variable (i.e., a moderator variable)? ➤ moderation analysis.

2. If you find no relationship between a predictor and an outcome variable: is it plausible to assume that there is a 'hidden effect' – that means, an effect which is contingent upon a third variable (i.e., a moderator variable)? ➤ moderation analysis.

3. Do you have reason to expect that the relationship between a predictor and an outcome is carried through another variable (i.e., a mediator variable)? ➤ mediation analysis.

 Traps

Analytics traps

- Overlooking a 'hidden effect': wrongfully concluding that there is no effect when in fact a moderator variable influences the relationship between two things.

- Using the same strategy or approach for your target audience without realising that some audience members are more responsive to another strategy or approach (i.e., failure to consider moderator variables).

- Stating a relationship between two things without understanding the underlying explanatory mechanisms and processes (i.e., failure to capture and engage with mediator variables).

Communication traps

- Speaking of moderation or mediation without explaining what these concepts mean and what a moderator or mediator 'does'.

- Removing visualisations that would substantially help your audience understand your data analysis and your findings.

Further resources

Find a helpful video on the difference between moderators and mediators at:

https://www.youtube.com/watch?v=WZr1jlKi_s0

To visualise moderation effects, go to this website and download the (free) Stats Tools Package and click on the '2 way interactions' tab:

http://statwiki.gaskination.com/index.php?title=Main_Page

Chapter

5

Segmenting the world: Differences that make a difference

What you'll learn

In this chapter, you will see how a statistical procedure called *cluster analysis* can help you group people, products or any other things based on (quantifiable) similarity. This lets you come up with targeted marketing strategies or helps you group employees who might need similar training. Cluster analysis is one of the most widely used unsupervised machine learning techniques; that means it requires no prior training data to do its job properly. You can use it for the automatic analysis of emails, photos, books, social media posts or customer surveys. There are different clustering methods, depending on the type, size and structure of the data. All of them, however, have certain benefits and drawbacks associated with them. So, having a basic understanding of clustering is helpful to use analytics results more judiciously (as they can vary dramatically).

As Herbert Simon, the only management scholar who ever won a Nobel prize in economics, put it: 'An early step toward understanding any set of phenomena is to learn what kinds of things there are in the set – to develop a taxonomy'. But how do you develop a taxonomy and why do you need one?

Well, the *how* is what this chapter is all about, namely cluster analysis – what Google and Amazon use to organise their data or to offer you recommendations. Cluster analysis is an iterative algorithm to group items based on their similarity regarding any number of given features (Figure 5.1).

The *why* should become clear if you look at the dialogue box below. We need taxonomies (what we call a classification that has been

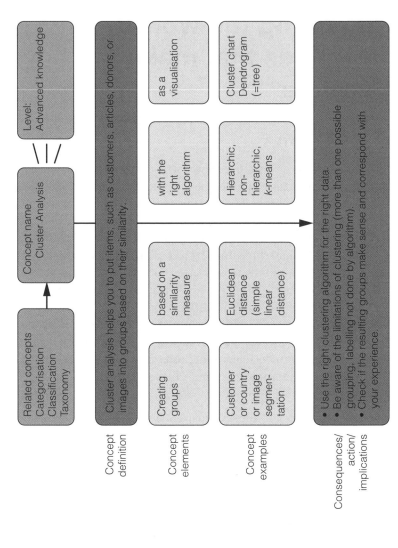

Figure 5.1 Key concepts to understand cluster analysis.

calculated quantitatively) whenever we have too many things to cater to (Bailey, 1994). It is easier, to pick up on the example above, to adapt e-mail messages to 12 different groups of clients than to 30,000 individual clients. Typical business applications of clustering are market segmentation, i.e., grouping people by their purchasing power, values, age, cultural backgrounds or past spending, to name but a few possibilities. Another application would be a risk-based segmentation where you could group your customers based on their credit history, for example. But clustering is also used in contexts such as HR, operations, insurance, project management (to cluster similar projects), in real estate (to find similar houses) or in urban planning. In these contexts, the power of this approach helps to distinguish meaningful groups of people, problems, projects, accidents, locations, houses or even regions based on key characteristics.

Data conversation

Josh's organisation has grown enormously over the last three years. Josh is the proud founder and CEO of a charity-oriented e-commerce site with now more than 30,000 clients who order anything from ecologically friendly coffee cups to blankets on his online shop. In light of an upcoming holiday, Josh is wondering how he should communicate with these clients, as they range widely in terms of age, spending, country of residence and product preferences. To make sense of his current customer groups, he is asking his analyst Rose to come up with a customer segmentation 'that makes sense based on their characteristics and purchasing behaviour thus far and that the marketing and sales team can then use to tailor Christmas messages to each segment'.

Rose is thrilled by this mission and tells Josh that she will run a cluster analysis on their internal customer database. Josh is happy that there is a method for his requests and has high hopes for the results.

When Rose presents her findings, however, he is anything but happy: Rose shows him 12 different customer groups and cannot pinpoint the one factor that distinguishes each group from another one. She even seems a bit unsure if the groups that she

▶

proposes are really the right segmentation. So, Josh decides that he should probe deeper and ask Rose in the next meeting what she has done to get to those groups and if the results from the cluster analysis could not be interpreted differently.

To do that, however, he believes he should first get a better understanding of clustering himself before confronting Rose. She has already thrown in a lot of jargon in their first discussion, and he had no idea why she brought up dendro-somethings and an old Greek geometer (Euclid), square roots and sums and even talked about the *Matrix*.

Broadly speaking, clustering helps us to deal with complexity and variety, and the mere mass of data or items. It helps us to literally see similarities and differences among things at one glance.

A cluster is basically any group of similar objects, whether its customers, houses, cities, donors, patients, products, risks or locations. But how, you may now ask, do I get to my clusters so that I can use them for planning, training, marketing or other purposes? How can I use the power of cluster analysis to segment my customers, group my photos, or find new market niches? These questions are answered in the next section where we describe the clustering process and the different kinds of clustering algorithms, as well as their application areas.

How clustering works

It is important to understand how clustering works, to interpret its results correctly, whether in marketing research, HR analytics, R&D or in other application areas. Creating groups based on their degree of similarity with regard to certain features is an iterative process, where certain steps have to be repeated by the computer to get it right. So even the computer cannot do this in one go. And it will not be able to do it alone, it needs you (yes you!) to give it some guidance and common sense in the process and come up with descriptive labels for the groups it has found.

You can let the program find the best clusters iteratively by giving it a suggested number of clusters to create and instructing it to find the best midpoint for that data cluster and then begin the process anew. This is called the k-means clustering approach. The letter 'k' designates the number of suggested segments or groups. An alternative to this would be to use a hierarchic clustering algorithm, where the computer starts building groups either from individual items to larger groups or vice versa. k-means is great for big data, while hierarchic cluster methods give you more flexibility as to how granular you want the groups to be (and it gives you really cool graphic representations called dendrograms).

Whatever mechanism you choose to build groups out of data, the ultimate number of groups may depend on your judgement call (and on the similarity measure that you chose) and what you believe is the most useful segmentation. There are certain rules of thumb for how many clusters make sense though. For example, if you jump from say five groups to four and notice that the variance within a cluster suddenly becomes a lot greater, you may want to stick with the initial five groups.

Summing up, here are the key steps you need to go through to group data with the help of cluster analysis:

1. Choose the data items that you want to group, such as customers or donors.

2. Gather data about those items (such as your customers' or donors' age, spending, location etc.). In other words, choose the variables that you want to use as clustering criteria.

3. Choose a way to calculate similarity (more on this in the following section).

4. Choose a clustering algorithm that finds items that are similar and groups them together.

5. Let it run (for a couple of times and perhaps with different clustering methods).

6. Examine the results and see if they make sense to you. For this step you may want to visualise the results of the cluster analysis (more on this option later).

7. If they do, give the resulting group informative names or labels that capture their essential traits (or how to deal with the respective group).

8. Devise measures to deal with the groups that have emerged (such as a segmented communication approach).

Simple enough, right? Key to this process, however, is *quantifying similarity*. Let's look at how this is done now so that you can understand what it really means to segment customers, employees, projects, or any other set of things.

What is similarity – statistically speaking?

As you have gathered by now, the whole notion of segmentation centres around the concept of similarity. It is thus helpful to develop a deeper understanding of what similarity really means in statistics and data science. A good place to start to build that understanding is the so-called Jaccard coefficient or index (then we will move on to another one called Euclidean distance).

The Jaccard index, also known as 'Intersection over Union' or the Jaccard similarity coefficient is a metric used to compare the similarity of certain sample sets (Jaccard, 1912). It is defined as the size of the overlap divided by the size of all of the data of the sample sets, or visually speaking, the fraction shown in Figure 5.2.

The Jaccard coefficient is a very simple quantification of similarity among sets. It can be used to detect plagiarism, or for other text mining purposes. A value of 40 per cent, for example, would indicate that the items in a group share 40 per cent of all their features.

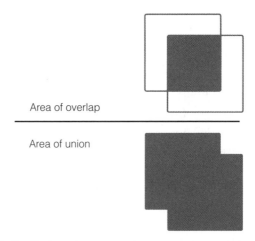

Area of overlap

Area of union

Figure 5.2 Similarity of two sample sets as the ratio between overlap (identical elements) and union (all of the elements).

They are identical with regard to 40 per cent of their attributes but differ with regard to 60 per cent of them. Think of the members of a family and their visual traits like hair, eye colour, nose shape, or height etc. In the case of a family with a Jaccard coefficient of, say, 20 per cent, we can hardly tell that they are related. With a Jaccard coefficient of 80 per cent, we see at one glance that they must be part of the same family.

The Jaccard coefficient is quite a restricted way to compare entire groups regarding their members. For many other applications, however, we need a more versatile measure of similarity, a so-called *distance metric* (to express degrees of similarity). With a single variable, similarity is super simple: the smaller the difference regarding a variable (say age of a customer), the more similar items (the customers) are. Or another example: two individuals are similar in terms of purchasing power, if their income level has a small difference and the level of dissimilarity increases as their income difference increases.

Now multiple variables (or features of comparison) require an aggregate distance measure. As we compare items along many attributes, such as income, age, consumption habits, gender, it becomes more difficult to define similarity with a single value. For this, we have a handy little formula that helps you summarise the differences along various features.

The most famous measure of distance is the Euclidean distance, which is the concept we use in everyday life for straight line distances (think of a direct flight line between two cities). It is important to understand how this measure of similarity comes about, so that you understand what a data scientist really means when he or she says 'we grouped similar data'. So, bear with us for a minute and try to digest the following formula.

To calculate this distance, you take the differences between the individual attributes and sum them up. You actually first square each difference so that negatives drop out and don't affect the sum of the differences. You then get rid of this square again by taking the square root at the end. This gives us a neat little formula for calculating the similarity of any given data:

$$D_{ij} = \sqrt{\sum_{k=1}^{n}(x_{ki} - x_{kj})^2} \quad \textit{Euclidean distance}$$

A⟍
⟍B

This basically means that we can express the many differences between two things as the distance between two points. This distance is made up of all the differences among the two things summed up. So Euclidean distance between two things can be expressed as the sum of their attributes' differences and that squared so that negatives do not play a role anymore. We sum up all the absolute differences, in other words.

Let us take a simple example to bring this formula alive:

Say we have four customers, and we compare them according to the money that they spend on our e-commerce shop in total per year.

	Money spent
Client 1	400
Client 2	150
Client 3	420
Client 4	100

So, calculating their differences pairwise would give us these values:

Client 1 vs Client 2	$400 - 150 = 250$
Client 1 vs Client 3	$400 - 420 = -20$
Client 1 vs Client 4	$400 - 100 = 300$
Client 2 vs Client 3	$150 - 420 = -270$
Client 2 vs Client 4	$150 - 100 = 50$
Client 3 vs Client 4	$420 - 100 = 320$

The numbers on the right express the differences among the customers in terms of their spending. We see that client 1 and client 3 are very similar, whereas clients 1 and 2, as well as 1 and 4 are very different.

Now money spent may not be enough to create a good grouping of these clients, so we also have a look at their age next:

	Money spent	Age
Client 1	400	55
Client 2	150	37
Client 3	420	64
Client 4	100	29

To combine the age differences with the spending differences, we should use the formula we have just learned on the previous page. Doing these gives us these values:

Client 1 vs Client 2	$\sqrt{(400 - 150)^2 + (55 - 37)^2} = 250$
Client 1 vs Client 3	$\sqrt{(400 - 420)^2 + (55 - 64)^2} = 22$
Client 1 vs Client 4	$\sqrt{(400 - 100)^2 + (55 - 29)^2} = 301$
Client 2 vs Client 3	$\sqrt{(150 - 420)^2 + (37 - 64)^2} = 271$
Client 2 vs Client 4	$\sqrt{(150 - 100)^2 + (37 - 29)^2} = 50$
Client 3 vs Client 4	$\sqrt{(420 - 100)^2 + (64 - 29)^2} = 322$

Ta-da! We have just quantified multidimensional similarity. We now see that when taking both attributes into account clients 3 and 4 are the most different from one another, whereas clients 1 and 3 are the most similar to each other. This will help us target measures or marketing messages at this *group* of clients, and not at each client individually.

We can now use these values to map out the so-called Euclidean (or direct) distance between the customers and create groups based on this relative positioning of all clients (actually, the computer will do this for us with the help of the calculated distance measures above). In reality, we would of course do this with many more customers than just three and with many more dimensions than just spending and age. We also might use another (or an additional) distance measure than the Euclidean one. But you get the point.

Please note that the choice of the preferred similarity measure will affect your results (i.e., the groups the computer generates). Clustering analysis in practice often requires sensitivity analysis to see whether the clustering results remain stable when you switch from Euclidean distance to another similarity measure. So testing for the robustness of your clusters is always a good idea. Switch your distance measures and see if this leads to other groups.

Visualising groups

How does the computer now work with these similarity values? In the case of hierarchic cluster analysis (where you first build larger groups that are then split into smaller ones), it calculates a so-called similarity matrix – that's the matrix Rose was mentioning to Josh – where the pairwise comparisons of differences are mapped out in a huge table.

The similarity matrix is sometimes also referred to as a distance matrix (as the values in it are the 'distance' between items, as calculated above). Based on this matrix (whose values are usually normalised to fall between 0 = no similarity to 1 = identical), the computer can calculate likely groupings. Note that other clustering algorithms, such as k-means, do not use this pointwise distance to calculate groups, but rather other measures such as means and deviations from the mean (for initially stipulated groups).

We can display the distances in a similarity or distance matrix visually in what is called a *dendrogram*, a simple tree diagram where the length of a branch indicates the distance between clusters (or items at its lowest level). Figure 5.3 shows an example of a simple dendrogram.

This dendrogram tells you that customers 3 and 1 are more similar to each other than to customers 3 and 4. It also tells you that the similarity between 3 and 1 is actually slightly bigger than the similarity between customers 2 and 4: the lower the items (or splits) on the dendrogram, the more similar they are, the higher the branching the less similar the items or groups are.

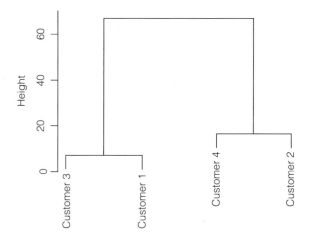

Figure 5.3 A simplified version of a dendrogram.

In reality, dendrograms look a lot more complicated than the above example and it's not always easy to decide at which level to cut the tree and build a group. In the example above it is clear that we can create two clusters, one consisting of customers 3 and 1, and a second cluster consisting of customers 2 and 4. Let's now examine the next, more realistic dendrogram. Where do you define the clusters here? A good rule is to cut wherever there is the most white space between branches. In the dendrogram below, this would give us just four main clusters. If useful, however, you can also use sub-clusters later for other purposes. That is the advantage of hierarchic clustering (and that you don't need to specify how many clusters you want upfront like in the k-means approach). Its disadvantage is that it is often cumbersome (and a bit slow) for really big data sets. It is also particularly sensitive to outliers, although they can usually be spotted well when you look at the resulting dendrogram. For extremely large data sets, the dendrogram can also lose a bit of its clarity and become cluttered and hard to read (Figure 5.4).

There are other ways to display distances, such as in a 3D space or on a simple plane. The latter visualisation would look like the figure in Figure 5.5 (right). The technical term for this graph would be a multidimensional scaling plot or a (self-organising) similarity map.

In our work with managers, however, we found that dendrograms often lead to more fruitful data discussions than the plot on the

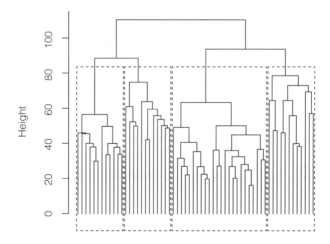

Figure 5.4 A more realistic dendrogram and its resulting groups.

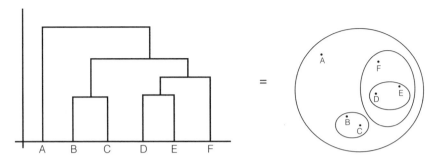

Figure 5.5 Two ways of displaying the results of cluster analysis: dendrogram (left) and similarity map (right).

right, as they found the tree a more natural way to browse groups and levels. Unfortunately, though, many visual analytics packages, like Tableau or Power BI, only give you the result displayed on the right and cannot generate a dendrogram. Please note that there are no cartesian coordinates (there is no x- or y-axis) on the graphic on the right and that the only thing that counts is the direct distances among the items A to F (so D is more similar to E than F is to A). It may be a good exercise to visually inspect and compare the two graphs and see if you understand that they are equivalent (Figure 5.5).

⚠ **How to say it**

Help people in interpreting clustering charts correctly

Be careful when you are showing dendrograms or similarity maps to others, as they can be easily misinterpreted (or overly cluttered). Be sure to explain that in a dendrogram the forkings represent different groupings of items and that the lower a forking happens, the more similar items are below it.

When showing a similarity map, you should emphasise that this type of chart does not have proper (horizontal and vertical) x- and y-axes. You ought to emphasise that the only meaningful information is the direct (flight) distance between items to represent their degree of similarity or difference.

Caveats for clustering

Before we get all too enthusiastic about the cool application possibilities of clustering, there are several caveats that we need to be aware of when segmenting data with the help of cluster analysis. Even as a manager, you should be aware of the risks and limitations of this grouping approach as they affect the ultimate result and its implications. Here are the top three limitations of cluster analysis.

1. Cluster analysis will not always give you clear cut groups. You need to try different algorithms, different numbers of groups, or different levels and apply your experience to find the grouping that is right for your data scope and application context. Ask your data scientists how well the items really fit the cluster they are assigned to by checking that the so-called silhouette scores are closer to 1 than to 0. The silhouette value simply is a measure of how similar an object is to its own cluster compared to other clusters. If many points have a low or negative value, then the clustering may have too many or too few clusters.

2. The computer does not come up with an explicit rationale or with descriptive *labels* for the groups that it has created. You will have to use your common sense and experience to diagnose the underlying patterns in the clusters. The clusters will not always be organised in the most action-oriented manner, so working with different versions (clustering approaches, similarity measures, levels, or number of groups) may help you find the best segmentation.

3. As with many other statistical analyses, (hierarchical) cluster analysis is sensitive to *outliers*. So, make sure you analyse the role of outliers in your data set. Try running a cluster algorithm also with a version of your data set where the outliers have been deleted. See if this impacts the created groups.

A word of caution also regarding the scope of this method, as cluster analysis is not your go-to method for all things grouped. In fact, you may want to distinguish cluster analysis from other statistical procedures, such as dimension reduction or factor analysis. The latter is also important in HR, marketing or sales.

It's useful to distinguish cluster analysis from other 'segmentation' techniques in this context. Remember that cluster analysis is used to group cases (things, customers, products) whereas *factor analysis* or *principal component analysis* (PCA) attempts to group features – characteristics or traits (such as size, volume, frequency etc.) that belong to one dimension for example. They are thus 'dimensionality reduction' techniques. Factor analysis (a very popular statistical technique) assumes the existence of *latent* or hidden factors underlying the observed data, whereas PCA tries to identify variables that are composites of the observed variables. So, if you want to group customers, your best bet is probably cluster analysis. If, however, you want to find out which factors relate to similar customer behaviour, then you might use one of the other techniques.

Cluster analysis, as mentioned earlier, is an example of *unsupervised* machine learning, as it is based on iteration and an examination of best fitting results and not on previously labelled training data (as in supervised machine learning). Because of this, you need to take the results of cluster analysis with a grain of salt and test them against your own judgement or experience, especially regarding group boundaries. You can care less about factor analysis as it is more of a behind the scenes tool for your data analyst than a front-end data torturing tool. Cluster analysis is typically used for such areas as customer segmentation, where an optimal solution is not guaranteed. You would need factor analysis, for example, if you would like to devise a personality test.

Having seen the benefits, types, procedures, visualisations, and caveats of cluster analysis, we can now return to Josh and Rose and how their data discussion turned out eventually.

Data conversation (continued)

Josh now digs cluster analysis and feels prepared for a follow-up conversation with Rose.

He thanks Rose again for the analysis and asks: 'Which clustering algorithm did you use and why?' Rose answers that she used hierarchic cluster analysis. Josh thus asks Rose if she could show him the dendrogram that resulted from the cluster analysis algorithm. When Rose shows him the tree diagram, he realises that there was a simpler solution than the 12 groups mentioned by Rose. At a higher level of the dendrogram, there is a grouping that consists of just four groups. When Josh asks Rose why she suggested 12 groups instead of four she says: 'I thought about that as well but then it seemed too simplistic and that the groups were a bit heterogenous that way, especially because of the outliers in each group, but it could still work for communicating to the customers'.

Josh and Rose first eliminate a few outliers, examine the new results, and then reduce the number of clusters to just four. They jointly find good names for each group (the hyperactive, the focused value shoppers, the occasional visitors, and the very passive) which helps to instruct the communication team on the specificities of each group and how to address them in their subsequent communication. They also analyse the outliers in each of the four groups and decide to address them separately.

Rose is as stunned at the end of the meeting as she is intellectually satisfied. Not only did she underestimate her boss's data literacy, but also how much value a good data dialogue can bring to the business. She is glad that Josh and her 'tortured' the data (as Josh called this) till it spoke to them more clearly.

Key take-aways

Whenever you need to make sense of data and think that grouping may be a good approach, ask yourself the following questions:

1. When looking at the results of a cluster analysis, ask yourself if this is the only way the group boundaries can be drawn? Does it correspond to your experiences; does it make sense? Could you reduce the number of groups for your purposes?

2. Are there outliers? What do we know about them? How do they affect the built groups?

3. What is the right number of groups for our purposes when we look at the dendrogram in detail?

4. How can we label the resulting groups in an informative manner, perhaps indicating how to actually deal with each respective group?

5. What is the best way to communicate the groups to your colleagues? If you have used hierarchical cluster analysis, think about showing a dendrogram. If you have used *k*-means or other non-hierarchic clustering algorithms, think about using a similarity map.

6. Am I grouping *items* or rather *features*? If I want to group features, such as personality traits or product characteristics, then factor analysis is the right choice. If you want to group elements, such as clients or products, then clustering algorithms are the right approach.

 Traps

Analytics traps

Possible risks with regard to cluster analysis are:

- Taking the results of the clustering for granted without conducting a sanity check or common-sense validation of the resulting groups.

- Using a clustering approach when factor analysis would be the right method because you want to group features (think personality traits) and not items (think customers or employees).

- Giving the groups non-descriptive labels that do not give a sense of the group items' characteristics.

- Not understanding the impact of the chosen similarity measure on the final grouping. Hence, be sure to ask for a sensitivity analysis of the type of similarity measures used. That means that the analysts show you the impact (on the resulting groups) of using another similarity measure.

- A lack of data preparation that can greatly affect your clustering results (such as standardising versus not standardising the input variables). So ask whether data preparation has been done judiciously (and how).

Communication traps

- Don't dive right into the details of the clustering algorithm that you used and why it is the right one, but first set the scene with regard to overall purpose.

- Make sure you use an interactive version of a dendrogram when using it in a live presentation. This will allow you to show the different possible groups that can emerge from a cluster analysis.
- Pro-actively mention the limitations of the clustering method.

Further resources

A simple YouTube tutorial on four of the most important clustering techniques:

https://www.youtube.com/watch?v=Se28XHI2_xE

A great and concise book that also covers cluster analysis in a succinct matter:

Bailey, K.D. (1994) *Typologies and taxonomies: An introduction to classification techniques.* Sage.

Chapter

Detecting data distortions: Analytics biases that everyone should know

What you'll learn

In this chapter we discuss frequently made mistakes in the analytics process. These so-called biases affect the quality of analytics-based decision making negatively and should thus be recognised and avoided.

Like most of you, we trust our intuition in areas where we have lots of experience, but we rather rely on data where we don't. In the latter case, we feel more secure and confident when we have relevant data. However, caution is warranted as the mere availability of data may give us a false sense of security.

So, whenever there is relevant data, we feel that our decision making must improve.

But that ain't necessarily so.

Sometimes data is the very reason why we make a wrong decision.

Why? Because data, its analysis, or the way that it is communicated or used may be severely *biased* or misleading (Figure 6.1). That is the bad news.

The good news is that you can cultivate a healthy scepticism against data biases: you can detect or even prevent such distortions. You can immunise your analytics endeavours against these recurring thinking errors.

How? By knowing about them, by recognising them in your analytics work, by understanding (and addressing) their root causes and, of course, by knowing their remedies. See if you can already recognise a few problematic aspects in the short dialogue below.

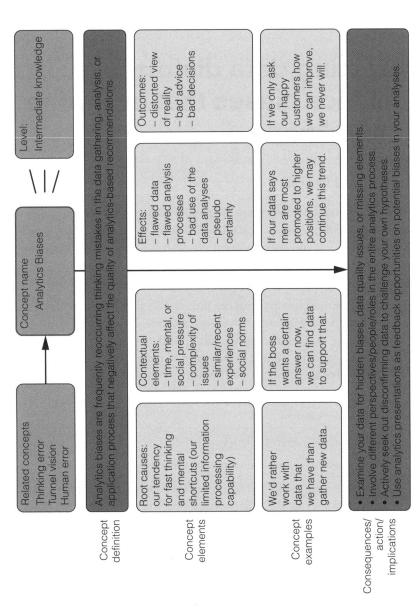

Figure 6.1 Key concepts of analytics biases.

Related concepts	Thinking error Tunnel vision Human error
Concept name	Analytics Biases
Level:	Intermediate knowledge

Concept definition: Analytics biases are frequently reoccurring thinking mistakes in the data gathering, analysis, or application process that negatively affect the quality of analytics-based recommendations.

Concept elements:

Root causes: our tendency for fast thinking and mental shortcuts (our limited information processing capability)

Contextual elements:
– time, mental, or social pressure
– complexity of issues
– similar/recent experiences
– social norms

Effects:
– flawed data
– flawed analysis processes
– bad use of the data analyses
– pseudo certainty

Outcomes:
– distorted view of reality
– bad advice
– bad decisions

Concept examples:

We'd rather work with data that we have than gather new data.

If the boss wants a certain answer now, we can find data to support that.

If our data says men are most promoted to higher positions, we may continue this trend.

If we only ask our happy customers how we can improve, we never will.

Consequences/action/implications:
- Examine your data for hidden biases, data quality issues, or missing elements.
- Involve different perspectives/people/roles in the entire analytics process.
- Actively seek out disconfirming data to challenge your own hypotheses.
- Use analytics presentations as feedback opportunities on potential biases in your analyses.

Data conversation

John is a junior risk analyst in an insurance company. He is reporting to Beth who runs the analytics team of the firm. There is a request from a risk management team who recently detected a slight increase in claims (i.e., reported damages to cover by the insurance) for one group of individual customers and wants to understand why that is. Having looked at the data, John schedules a meeting with Beth to discuss this request and his findings thus far.

John: I'm glad that we get the chance to talk about that case of the spiking damages, Beth.

Beth: Yes, me too, tell me more about it. I only read the e-mail from the risk management team that has noticed the increase in claims.

John: When I got their claims data, I remembered reading an article last week about how the lockdown may lead to more domestic accidents. So, I suspected this might be the cause here as well and started looking at corona-related causes in those claims. I was quite sure that many of the damages were related to the quarantine and to activities that happen when you stay in your home office and guess what: I found quite a few of them. So, I looked at clients whose job was directly affected by the pandemic and indeed I found that many of them had claims related to accidents while working at home. I even ran a regression on that data set and the R-squared values were excellent, which kind of proves my point. There is a corona premium that we are paying out due to increased home office work and thus increased domestic accidents. I see a clear causal chain there, more time at home leads to more accidents at home. Perhaps we should advise the communication team to run a campaign on 'how to keep your home office safe'.

Beth: Wait just a minute here, John. Haven't you focused a bit too much and too early on just corona there as a cause of

▶

> the rise in claims? Couldn't there be other reasons why the claims went up?
>
> *John:* Well, the data I collected is quite clear on that point: home office is the culprit.
>
> *Beth:* John, I want you to re-do the analysis on this. This time be as broad and open minded as possible and look out for data that contradicts your hypothesis that the increase in claims is due to increased home office work. Look at other clients as well who also work from home and whose claims have not gone up, okay? Look at contractual differences, at the demographics and the rest.
>
> *John:* Um, okay boss, I'll get right to it. Only the paranoid survive, I guess.

Did you recognise the hidden biases in John's work? Maybe this will help.

Figure 6.2 presents ten crucial biases in the analytics process. If you are using data in HR processes, in risk assessment, in marketing or sales, in controlling or in credit approval, then you want to make sure you are steering clear of these ten analytics pitfalls. In these contexts, any of the three biases outlined below can lead to decision fiascos, as biased data may lead you to wrong recommendations.

The biases are structured along the *data gathering, data analysis and data application* (i.e., communication and usage) process. We had three main reasons for choosing our list of ten crucial biases from the large group of biases (see our interactive map at bias.visual-literacy.org for more than 180 of them).

- We have seen that they occur *frequently* in the analytics process of many organisations.
- They have a *big negative impact* on the quality of analytics and the subsequent decisions.
- They can be prevented as effective *countermeasures* exist against them.

In the following section, we discuss why these biases happen (their root causes), how you can recognise them (the symptoms) and of

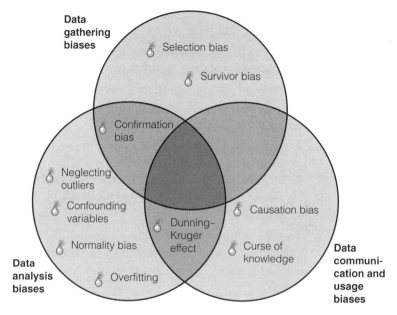

Figure 6.2 Ten analytics biases every professional should know.

course how to fight them (their remedies) to improve the quality of data analytics (Figure 6.2).

1. Data gathering biases

It sounds paradoxical, but one of the biggest mistakes that you can make in analytics is simply *working with the data that you have.*

It's like in the story of the man searching for his keys under a streetlight. A passenger asks him whether he is sure that he has lost them there, to which the man replies: 'No, I lost them over there, but the lighting is much better over here'. So just because you have data, doesn't mean that it's the right one for your decision.

When looking for data, be aware of three specific biases that may distort your data sourcing: our tendency to use *conveniently available* data instead of the right data, our tendency to look at data that was *completed* rather than data that is still missing (think of customer surveys), and our tendency to seek data that *confirms* our initial opinion. Here is our snapshot of each data gathering bias.

- **Selection bias**

  - Description: our tendency to use conveniently available data instead of representative data (e.g., the participants in a study differ systematically from the population of interest).

  - Root causes: time pressure, laziness, budget constraints, technical constraints.

  - Symptoms: skewed data that does not represent the full spectrum of the underlying population (e.g., overly positive product evaluations), gaps between expected outcomes (e.g., successful product launch) and reality (e.g., the product flops).

  - Remedies: examine your sampling approach and the inclusion/exclusion criteria that you apply, use randomisation methods when selecting items from your population of interest.

- **Survivor bias**

  - Description: focusing on the results that came through and ignoring what has not. For example, only analysing completed customer surveys, and ignoring those that have not been fully completed.

  - Root causes: important data collection opportunities were overlooked, barriers to data completion at the source, cumbersome data entering process.

  - Symptoms: data is skewed (for example, only happy customers or really upset clients have answered the survey), gaps between expected outcomes and reality.

  - Remedies: follow-up on data sources that did not yield data and find alternative ways to achieve completion. If possible, make the data entering process a more seamless experience.

- **Confirmation bias**

  - Description: data analysts sometimes only seek data to confirm their (or their manager's) opinions.

  - Root causes: social/peer pressure, opinionated mindset, overly homogenous analytics team, time pressure.

  - Symptoms: data corresponds perfectly to one's own hypotheses ('too good to be true').

- Remedies: actively seek out contradictory data. Split up the data gathering and/or analysis tasks among two independent teams. Ask for data or variables that have been excluded from the analysis.

2. Data analysis biases

Once you have de-biased your data gathering approach, make sure that you also immunise your data analysis against typical *statistical biases*. These classic statistics blunders are not just the result of sloppy thinking. They may also result from a naïve treatment of data, or an overly narrow analysis focus. Here are our top four data analysis biases.

- Confounding variables
  - Description: not taking forces – i.e., variables – into account that affect the association between two things (i.e., resulting in a mixing of effects). Thinking that a drives b, just because a and b move in the same direction (e.g., swimming pool visits may not drive ice cream sales, as both are driven by hot temperatures).
  - Root causes: incomplete hypotheses or models.
  - Symptoms: spurious associations among variables; no observed association, although it would be reasonable to assume that there is one.
  - Remedies: measure and report all variables that might affect an outcome, include potential confounding variables in your analyses, provide adjusted estimates for associations after the effects of the confounder have been removed.

- Neglecting outliers
  - Description: not acknowledging outliers (radically different items in a sample) at all or simply eliminating them.
  - Root causes: exotic or extreme items in data sets that go unchecked.
  - Symptoms: when you plot your data, you see a few items that are far apart from the rest.
  - Remedies: identify outliers and their impact on the data's descriptive statistics, use appropriate measures of central tendency (e.g., median instead of mean), run analyses without the outliers and compare results.

- **Normality bias**

  - Description: not taking the actual distribution of the sample into account (for example, an employee survey where most employees are quite happy with their working conditions).

  - Root causes: assuming normal distribution for a data set (even if it's not a bell curve) and running statistical tests that are for normal distribution only (otherwise use non-parametric tests).

  - Symptoms: unreliable quality indicators for the statistical tests.

  - Remedies: examine the real frequency distribution of the sample and run the tests that are fit for that kind of distribution.

- **Overfitting**

  - Description: playing with models so that they fit the data we have, but not beyond it.

  - Root causes: a limited data sample, a model that is too specific.

  - Symptoms: a seemingly perfect model that accommodates all the available data perfectly, but is bad at predicting future observations (beyond the dataset).

  - Remedies: collect additional data to extend and re-validate the model, remove variables that do not really have a relationship with the outcome.

3. Data communication and usage biases

Data has no value if it is not properly communicated and used. The last step in the analytics process – communication and use – is thus of special importance. In this crucial step several things can go wrong. The data analysts could communicate their results badly (incomprehensibly using jargon) or the managers could misinterpret the results (because they overestimate their own data literacy or confuse correlation with causation).

- **Curse of knowledge**

  - Description: analysts fail to adequately communicate (simplify) their analyses to managers because they have forgotten how complex their procedures are.

- Root causes: lacking knowledge about target groups of analysis. Lacking data storytelling skills.
- Symptoms: puzzled looks on managers' faces, off-topic questions, lacking follow-up.
- Remedies: grandma test (how would you explain it to your grandmother?). Seek feedback from managers on what they find most difficult to understand. Communication training for data scientists.

- **Dunning–Kruger effect**

  - Description: managers overestimate their grasp of statistics at times and are unaware of their wrong data interpretation or use.
  - Root causes: overoptimism of managers regarding their own statistics understanding.
  - Symptoms: superficial data conversations.
  - Remedies: the first rule of the Dunning–Kruger club is that you don't know that you're a member of it, so enable managers to pre-test their data literacy and discover their knowledge gaps. Ask them challenging questions so that they can see the limitations of their own statistics know-how (in a face-saving way).

- **Causation bias**

  - Description: believing that one factor causes another, simply because the two are correlated (for example, employee fluctuations and sales).
  - Root causes: limited statistics understanding.
  - Symptoms: 'strange' relationships that contradict common sense, a design that does not allow for such inferences (e.g., because data was not gathered using strict experimental methods).
  - Remedies: inform managers about the difference between correlation and causation. Show the additional tests that need to be made to clarify causation (beyond correlation).

> ### ⚠ How to say it
>
> #### Reducing the curse of knowledge
>
> Try the following approaches to overcome the curse of knowledge and communicate analytics in an overly complex manner:
>
> - Try to find out how much your audience actually already knows about analytics, statistics, or the data that you are sharing with them. Why not meet one of your data consumers for an informal cup of coffee and assess their previous knowledge in this way?
> - Explain your data first in a one-on-one session with someone who never had to deal with them before and ask them for honest feedback on how clear you were. Ask him or her what others might find difficult hearing about this data for the first time.
> - Think about all the terms that you have used in describing the data that could have other meanings. Try to replace those words (such as robust, significant, bootstrapping, distribution etc.) with more specific ones or explain them further.
> - Make it extra easy for your data consumers to ask questions by encouraging them to do so at various points during a data presentation.

You now know ten of the most relevant biases in the analytics context. Use this knowledge wisely. Bust those biases, detect those distortions and control the quality of your data-based decision making.

Data conversation (continued)

John: Thanks Beth for this follow-up meeting opportunity. I must apologise. I really jumped to conclusions last time and fell in love with my hypothesis of corona being the cause of all evil. I was too selective in my analysis of the data

---

and just wanted to confirm my own hypothesis. It turns out something completely different caused the spike in claims that had nothing to do with home office work. The real driver of the increase is that for many of the clients with increased claims, their contractual conditions are about to change. So, it seems, that quite a few of them just wanted to profit from the old contract parameters and thus filed a claim just before their conditions changed. This happened across the board, including customers who did not work at home, but continued working in grocery stores etc.

Beth: Wow, so we scrap the 'safe home office campaign idea' and we should immediately advise our agents to carefully re-check that all these claims are really legitimate, right?

John: Exactly. It probably has no connection whatsoever with corona. Sorry about that Beth. It could be fraud in some of the cases. I just didn't think of that possibility as we had very few fraud incidences so far.

Beth: Well, when people are financially in dire straits, as many are now, this is actually more likely to happen. So, there is a corona connection after all, John, just not the one you were thinking of.

John: That is a small consolation. Next time before I check my data, I need to check my thinking, that's what I'm really taking away from this. And thank you for your scepticism, it made a huge difference and ultimately paid off.

So, inform both managers and data analysts about these risks and about their remedies and install safeguards or countermeasures wherever possible. First and foremost, however, protect yourself against the specific biases that are most likely to affect you. Shakespeare's following famous quote is a useful reminder for this last point:

'A fool thinks himself to be wise, but a wise man knows himself to be a fool'.

Key take-aways

Whenever you are dealing with data and its analysis, there are a few questions that are important to ask from a bias or distortion point of view:

1. Has the data selection been undertaken in an open manner and is it free of systematic bias?
2. Has the data analysis addressed disconfirming evidence, outliers, potential confounding variables, and non-normal distribution issues?
3. Has the data been properly understood and adequately used by the recipients? Has it become crystal clear what the data tells us and where its limitations are?

 ## Traps

Important risks to be aware of that can distort your data or the subsequent analysis are the following:

- Sampling risks: getting the wrong kind of data for your analysis.
- Analysis risks: conducting an analysis that is not accurate enough, distorted by outliers or too narrowly focused on a data-subset.
- Communication risks: conveying the risks in a (overly complicated and one-sided) way that leads to misunderstanding and misusing the data.

Further resources

Further biases with a relevance for analytics can be found at:

https://tinyurl.com/statsbiases

https://blogs.oracle.com/analytics/post/10-cognitive-biases-in-business-analytics-and-how-to-avoid-them

https://www.allerin.com/blog/avoiding-bias-in-data-analytics

https://medium.com/de-bijenkorf-techblog/cognitive-biases-in-data-analytics-b53ea3f688e4

A great article of our St Gallen colleagues on the key biases in machine learning can be found at:

https://aisel.aisnet.org/cgi/viewcontent.cgi?article=1166&context=wi2021

Part

2

Communicating data

Chapter

7

Asking the right questions about data

What you'll learn

This short chapter gives you a set of questions to ask data specialists when discussing analytics results. It will help you structure the questions and answers part after a data scientist has presented his or her data to the audience. We will show you three kinds of questions to ask and how to ask them in the most constructive way possible.

Data conversation

Ellen: . . . and this concludes my presentation of our monthly website traffic analysis. I'm now gladly available to answer any questions that you might have.

Harry: Thank you very much Ellen. Um, does anyone have any questions or should we move right on to the marketing plan at this point? We only have about 30 minutes left by the way for that.

Jennifer: Just a quick question Ellen: Will you send us these slides also electronically by e-mail?

Ellen: Sure, I can do that, they are already on our SharePoint server though.

Jennifer: Okay, it would still be nice if you could send them.

Ellen: Okay, I will.

Harry: Excellent. Any other issues? Well then, let's move on.

William: I'm sorry Harry, I don't want to slow us down, but I'm a bit confused. Ellen, didn't you say the data only covers

---

▶

the first half of the month because of server issues? And still, you made recommendations based on those two weeks that affect my department negatively. Plus, you seem to have compared an off-season month with a high-season one in some of your recommendations. This is all a big mess.

Ellen: Um, no we normalised the data for that actually.

William: Whatever. I don't think we should put your recommendations in the meeting minutes at this point.

Harry: O wow, I think we'll need a follow-up on this. Let's do this the three of us, okay? Now on to our marketing plan.

To be continued.

Slowly but surely analytics practices are taking hold in organisations and most professionals are becoming familiar with data-driven decision making. They are using customer data to better target their sales, operational data to streamline processes, HR data to finetune trainings, or sentiment analysis to understand their social media impact, to name but a few examples.

But to make such analytics efforts successful, *high-quality dialogues* between business professionals and their analytics colleagues are crucial.

In our experience, *asking the right questions about the data* and its analysis is a key task to get the maximum value out of data and analytics applications (Figure 7.1). To support teams in their collaboration, we have thus compiled particularly *useful questions that business people should ask their data scientists* whenever they are presented with new data or discuss analysis results together.

The questions that we found particularly helpful can be grouped into three areas.

1. Questions related to data sources and data quality.
2. Questions relating to the data analysis.
3. Application-related questions.

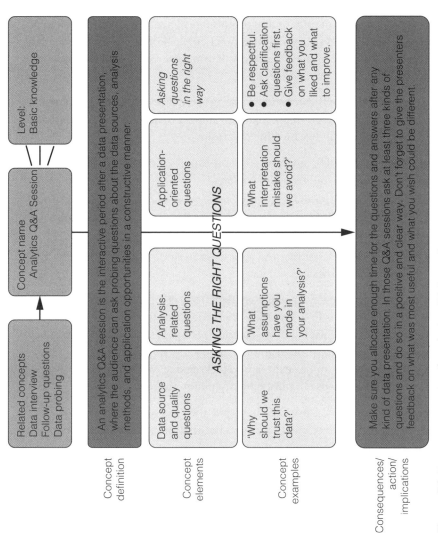

Figure 7.1 Key components of analytics Q&A sessions.

Concept name
Analytics Q&A Session

Level:
Basic knowledge

Related concepts
Data interview
Follow-up questions
Data probing

Concept definition

An analytics Q&A session is the interactive period after a data presentation, where the audience can ask probing questions about the data sources, analysis methods, and application opportunities in a constructive manner.

Concept elements

Data source and quality questions

Analysis-related questions

Application-oriented questions

Asking questions in the right way

Concept examples

'Why should we trust this data?'

'What assumptions have you made in your analysis?'

'What interpretation mistake should we avoid?'

- Be respectful.
- Ask clarification questions first.
- Give feedback on what you liked and what to improve.

ASKING THE RIGHT QUESTIONS

Consequences/ action/ implications

Make sure you allocate enough time for the questions and answers after any kind of data presentation. In those Q&A sessions ask at least three kinds of questions and do so in a positive and clear way. Don't forget to give the presenters feedback on what was most useful and what you wish could be different.

The first kind of questions are instrumental to better assess the *validity* and *reliability* of the data. The second set is helpful to understand what the data scientists have *actually done with the data (and why)*. This prepares the ground for the third type of questions: application-oriented questions are probably the most important ones to *turn insights into impact*. They enable you to put the analysis results into practice. Still, you can only assess the answers to these questions if you have first asked the other two types of questions.

What are the benefits of asking these three kinds of questions? Let us just mention the main advantages of adding these questions to your analytics meeting repertoire.

- They help analysts and non-experts build common ground and avoid *misunderstandings*.
- They improve the *rigour and relevance* of the data analysis, by providing focus, uncovering weak spots, and subsequently improving the data gathering and analysis process.
- They assist you and your team in finding *innovative* new ways to harness your data.

So how can you reap these benefits? Let's examine the repertoire of questions first, and then briefly describe the best way to use them. Read the list below as a menu to choose from. You will never have time to go through all of them in a meeting, nor is that even necessary. But in our experience, picking one to two questions per type makes sense in most data discussion forums.

For every group, we have put the questions in a sequence that makes sense and that allows the analyst to gradually open up (and not shut down or become defensive).

1. Questions related to data sources and data quality

Any analysis can only be as good as the underlying data. You must thus understand where the data came from and if it is *fit for use*. To *assess* the data sources and the quality of the data, you can ask your analytics colleagues the following five questions.

1. Why are you focusing on *this* data? What questions does it *answer* and why are these questions crucial for us? In other words: What's the *value* of this data?

2. Can you tell me how, where (sources and their reliability) and when (time period) we have gathered this data? What *biases*, events, assumptions or preferences may have affected this data gathering?

3. What do we know about the data's reliability, consistency, completeness and accuracy? Is the data *trustworthy* in your view and current enough?

4. What data are we *missing* that you wish we should have? Are there ways to get it?

5. How much is the gathering of this data *costing* us? Are there ways to make this cheaper, more automised (for example through AI)?

2. Questions related to the data analysis

Many data analysts love to talk about their techniques, tools and how they generally conduct their work. It is thus important to *focus* the discussion on the analysis parts that really matter for the subsequent use of the data. The following questions can help you to steer the conversation towards useful data analysis aspects.

1. What are the key *terms* and concepts that I really need to understand to make sense of this data? Please explain them to me as if I knew nothing about statistics.

2. What were the analytical tools, *procedures* and *assumptions* that you have applied to this data and why those and not others? Anything I should know about these procedures?

3. What *surprised* you when you did the analysis of this data?

4. What was the greatest *difficulty* in analysing this data?

5. What's the finding you're most sure about, and where do you have less certainty?

3. Application-related questions

Data should be a catalyst for decisions and actions. To help analysts turn data to decisions, ask them the following questions.

1. What's the *key finding* of your data analysis and why? What would you *do* in light of this data?

2. What results could be easily *misinterpreted or misused*? How so? Where should we be careful regarding the generalisability of our interpretations?

3. *Who else* should hear about these insights? What should they do with them?

4. Is there any other way we could exploit this data and get value out of it?

5. If we could start this data analysis over, what would you do *differently* now (to avoid errors, reduce cost, or answer additional questions or enable better application)?

A word of caution here: not all analysts see it as their role to make suggestions based on their data. Some see their job as mere data delivery and synthesis. This last set of questions should thus be asked carefully, iteratively and (most importantly) constructively (signalling respect and a willingness to improve together). Try to establish a collegiate atmosphere when talking about the data's uses. This brings us to the final section on *how* to ask analytics questions.

Asking questions constructively

Having outlined *which* questions you should ask in analytics meetings, let's now turn to *how* to best ask these questions. You certainly do not want your analytics staff (who may not always enjoy the communication side of their job) to become scared, defensive, or worried every time they meet you to discuss data insights. So, finding the right *tone, time, and tenacity* for your questions is imperative.

Your *tone* should be respectful, curious, and non-accusatory. The very advantage of the question format is that you are simply showing interest and want to know more, without casting a judgement or accusing somebody of not doing their job properly. Hence use the power of the (open) question format and avoid leading questions.

The *timing* of your questions should follow the process outlined above. So, start with simple, fact-based questions and gradually move to more complex and opinion-based ones. Also make sure that you time your questions well in the sense that you do not interrupt your analysts when they are presenting an issue that is clearly very important to them.

Regarding *tenacity* you should certainly challenge your analysts when they give you an evasive answer. At the same time, you should also show that you trust and respect them, for example when they have repeatedly given you the same kind of answer to a question.

Questions are of course not the only tool to use in such situations. As important as probing for data sources, analysis aspects, and decision consequences is *acknowledging* the work that has been done. So, don't forget to give positive feedback to your analytics staff (and listen to their feedback to you) and thank them for their efforts. Frame data discussions as *joint learning events* and track how you can improve them continuously. In this way you will avoid the most common source of mistakes in management, according to its most revered guru, Peter Drucker, who said:

'The most common source of mistakes in management decisions is the emphasis on finding the right answer rather than the right question'.

Data conversation (continued)

Harry: Thank you Ellen and William for this follow-up opportunity on our website analysis. I guess we should have probed these questions a bit earlier.

Ellen: I must say, with all due respect William, but you really made me look like a fool out there. I hope the marketing council will trust my presentation next month (sighs).

William: I'm sorry but it just didn't make sense to me to reduce my products' visibility on your homepage based on just two weeks' worth of website traffic data. How do we even know we can trust this data?

▶

Ellen:	Well, if you had asked me that, then I would have said that we cross-checked our findings with previous months, and they turned out to be consistent.
William:	How did you do that?
Ellen:	We ran a regression and also compared the results of earlier months with the two weeks' results from this month and it turned out that 'new products featured' was the best predictor for sales. So, we are quite confident that we need to regularly feature new products to engage customers to deep dive into our e-commerce store.
William:	Ah okay, I didn't know that's what that variable actually meant. I should have asked. I think we could also add a 'new products featured' to our subsite actually. Would that be in line with your findings?
Ellen:	Very much so but do make sure that they are highlighted as new again in the product listings further on. Our data shows that customers need that extra guidance. Otherwise, many of them give up too soon when scrolling through all the products.
William:	Got it!
Ellen:	Great question, by the way, I should have perhaps mentioned that in my presentation.
William:	It would be great if you could include such pointers in your next presentation.
Ellen:	Will do!
Harry:	My learning here is that we should definitely spend more time discussing our analytics findings. I'll allocate fifteen more minutes for Q&A next month. And thank you both for your openness here.

Key take-aways

Whenever there is a presentation of analytics or data among a group of people, make sure you reserve time for questions and answers. Pay special attention to these elements:

- Make the presenter feel comfortable and start with reassuring observations and appreciative questions.
- Make sure everyone has the same understanding. Ask questions that others might feel shy to ask.
- Start with clarification and fundamental questions before you enter detailed discussions.
- It is legitimate to ask questions about the reliability of the data sources and the trustworthiness of the data.
- Make sure you ask questions about the hidden assumptions that guided the data scientist's analysis work.
- Probe the analyst about the action implications of the data and the interpretation limits.
- Give constructive feedback that allows the data scientists to improve their data presentation next time around.

 ## Traps

Possible risks in data Q&A sessions are:

- Accusing the analysts of not doing their job properly, instead of helping them to improve their data delivery to decision makers.
- Creating an atmosphere where no one is willing to admit they did not understand the data.
- Having a pseudo or superficial understanding of presented data and asking only alibi questions (as Jennifer did in the opening dialogue).
- Offending or scaring data analysts so that they will no longer want to present in front of that audience.
- Asking leading questions that force the data scientist in a certain direction that the data itself may not warrant.

Further resources

Here are two great HBR articles on the power of asking questions:

https://hbr.org/2018/05/the-surprising-power-of-questions

https://hbr.org/2015/03/relearning-the-art-of-asking-questions

Here's another take on the questions to ask your analytics team:

https://knowledge.insead.edu/blog/insead-blog/are-you-asking-the-right-questions-of-your-data-team-17056

Chapter

8

How to visually design your data: A chart guide

What you'll learn

Visualise or vanish! To let data speak to your audience, you need to show it in graphic ways. In this chapter we present six simple principles (and a secret) to make your data visible in any situation and to avoid common data visualisation pitfalls in the management context.

Data conversation

'The Survey Meeting'

The moment has finally come: Arthur's time to shine. Having started in the marketing department about 6 months ago, this is his first major presentation. Arthur feels confident to be well prepared. He has put together a compact slide set summarising the latest customer survey.

Arthur: Good morning to you all, let's dive right into our latest client survey. I have visualised the demographics of the participants on this slide, I think it speaks for itself, so let's move on to the next slide.

Jennifer: Arthur, just a second, how come the numbers in that pie chart with the industry background of our customers add up to more than 100 per cent, that seems odd.

▶

Arthur: Oh, because in the customer survey they could actually choose more than one industry if they wanted. I guess I should have mentioned that.

Jennifer: Oh okay.

Arthur: On this next slide you see how the different types of customers rate us on different scales. The green line represents our commodity customers, the orange line our loyalty customers, the brown line our premium segment customers, the beige line our value customers, and the pink line our single-item customers, with the dotted line representing test clients. All packed into one line chart, pretty neat, eh?

Phil: This looks like my favourite pasta dish, a coloured spaghetti mash-up (everybody laughs).

Arthur: Yeah, it's a lot of lines, I know, sorry about that. Perhaps I should have split them up into different charts. Let's move to the next slide.

Jennifer: Sorry, what's the insight from your spaghetti chart?

Arthur: Oh yeah, generally that our customers are overall very happy with our after-sales service, but price sensitive customers aren't thrilled about our warranty parameters and duration.

Jennifer: Thanks. I can't really see the difference between the beige and the brown line in the end because of the grid and the legend. Are the values identical there?

Arthur: They are different, but you can't see it, sorry the labels there overlap. Moving right along, the next slide shows 12 pie charts that represent our portfolios of offerings for the various customer types and sub-types. I know you can't really see it here, but the service section is often the smallest one in the higher value segments.

Phil: Is that what we should focus on?

Arthur:	I guess we could grow our services with our premium segment, yes. In fact, my next slide shows that customers in that segment are not very familiar with our range of services. You can kinda see that in the smaller chunk in this doughnut chart here.
Phil:	That's the keyword right there: time for doughnuts and a coffee break. Arthur, can we have a word? (Phil approaches Arthur while everyone gets coffee and sweets.)

Listen Arthur, this is great data, but you made it awfully hard for us to absorb it.

Arthur:	But I visualised it.
Phil:	Yes, but it's hard to compare those pie segments. Plus, you haven't really directed our attention to what matters. I was distracted by the fancy shading, colouring, and 3D effects. Just lose that next time and focus on the numbers and their implications, would you?
Arthur:	Sure, I can do that.
Phil:	And Arthur, I do love spaghetti, but putting that many intersecting lines in a single chart makes no sense. And speaking of food: leave the doughnuts for coffee and try bar charts for those portfolio visualisations. I know you're going to present a deep-dive of the survey next week to our sales managers, why don't we have a quick look at those charts together before you present it to them?
Arthur:	Yes, let's do that Phil. Thanks

Almost everyone today is in the data business, whether you realise it or not. Hence, we all need to become competent in conveying data effectively to others, whether it is in a presentation, report, dashboard, as part of a website or in a simple conversation. But we live in a data-abundant world, where our data is constantly competing with other compelling facts for attention.

To improve our communication of data and ensure that it is noticed and understood, we can rely on a time-tested approach: data visualisation. In fact, visualising data offers a myriad of benefits, from improved attention, quicker communication, better retention, to deeper exploration, sustained motivation and stronger engagement with the data.

To reap these benefits, however, you need to pay attention to a few key principles that ensure that a picture really is worth a thousand words – and doesn't require a thousand words to become clear.

Having screened a plethora of books, articles and tutorials, and having conducted more than 50 data visualisation training sessions ourselves to managers from New York to Pretoria, from Bratislava to Bangalore, we have condensed the many data visualisation guidelines out there into just six memorable principles that anyone who visualises data for greater impact should consider.

These principles can be summarised with the DESIGN acronym that stands for the following six data visualisation imperatives (Figure 8.1).

Declutter
Emphasise
Storify
Involve
Give meaning
No distortions

The logic behind this set of principles is the following:

A high-quality data visualisation is one that is void of clutter or distraction, emphasises its main insight visually, tells a compelling story (with a 'so-what') and considers and captivates its audience. It gives clear meaning to numbers and avoids distortions or misinterpretations.

In the following, we put more meat on the bone of this acronym through varied examples and by providing a memorable tagline for each principle (Figure 8.2).

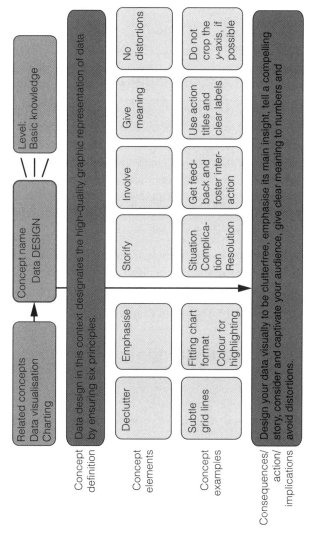

Figure 8.1 Key concepts for visualising data.

| Declutter | Emphasise | Storify | Involve | Give meaning | No distortions |

Figure 8.2 The six design principles for great data charts.

1. Declutter: The art of visual clarity

Decluttering a chart means eliminating everything that *distracts* from your data. So, get rid of borders, dominant grid lines, unnecessary details (such as decimals), 3D effects, (too many) colours, shades or other decoration effects (including exaggerated animation schemes). The following example (Figure 8.3) shows what you can leave out when visualising numbers. It is also an example of our next principle, emphasising key information visually (through a different colour or grey tone).

Also, make sure that your labels, legend or callouts do not interfere or overlap with the actual data display. A shocking counter example of this happened to *The Economist* magazine.[1]

So, remember this: When in doubt – leave it out.

2. Emphasise: Highlighting the main message of a chart

Emphasising means two things: first, that you choose the graphic format that best highlights your key insight or chart purpose

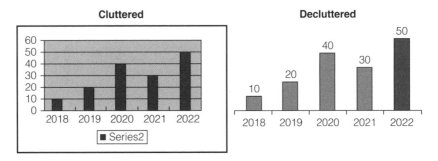

Figure 8.3 The original chart from Excel on the left, the decluttered and emphasised chart on the right.

(Figure 8.4). Second, that you emphasise the most important element in that chart visually, for example through a different colour or by circling it.

To choose the right chart format for your data content ask yourself the following questions:

- Do you want to enable *comparisons*? Then choose vertical bars.
- Do you want to enable a *ranking* from smallest to largest? Then choose horizontal bars.
- Do you want to show a *trend* over time? Then use a line chart.
- A last option would be to emphasise *deviations* from a goal or reference (such as a budget plan). In this case choose upwards and downwards vertical bars.

There are, of course, other purposes and formats beyond these four main ones. *Scatter plots* are a good way to emphasise correlations or distributions and *maps* are the right format for data with a geographical dimension. In our periodic table of visualisation methods,[2] you can find many chart formats with examples, but remember that your best bet is often the *bar chart*.

So: Don't look too far, just use the bar.

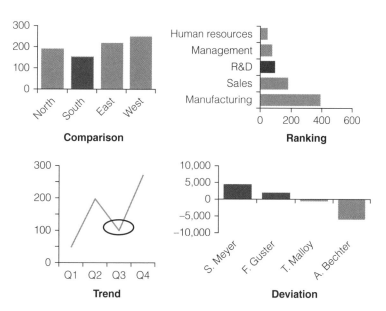

Figure 8.4 Four main data representation formats every manager should know.

3. Storify: Drama for your data

To storify data means to present a chart (or a series thereof) in a way that lets you tell a captivating tale about the numbers that you are showing. In another chapter, we argue that this requires splitting your charts into a trilogy: (1) setting the scene (an overview chart or set that clarifies the situation); (2) showing the complications (one or several charts to show more details) and (3) providing a resolution (i.e., charts that show opportunities for action). You will recognise the Shrek-style 'S' in our acronym above, which makes reference to our data storytelling chapter. Hopefully, you will also remember the data storytelling insights we mention there (such as creating common ground – think Shrek in his bath).

Here is an example for a storified *dashboard* about female representation in management that we often use in our seminars and training and that follows the three acts/trilogy approach (and adds a bit of drama with the big '0% change' figure in the middle). The first row clarifies the situation by showing that our company S has a female workforce that is below average and only 15 per cent of women in management. The second row shows more complications, namely that these 15 per cent are only in the lower management and that this has not changed in the last five years. The last row points to solutions, namely that to get more women to apply to management positions there needs to be more support and more flexible working conditions (Figure 8.5). You will learn more about this in the next chapter on data storytelling by the way, where we will use a variation of this data as an illustration as well.

Storytelling is all about sequencing a set of charts or animating and enriching a single chart.[3]

Storifying your chart also means adding *emotion* to it – if appropriate – and giving it a distinctive visual style. It means connecting with the audience by making the data relevant to them (selling before telling). This brings us to our next point: (audience) involvement. Before that, here's the tagline for principle number 3:

To give data glory, tell it in a three-part story.

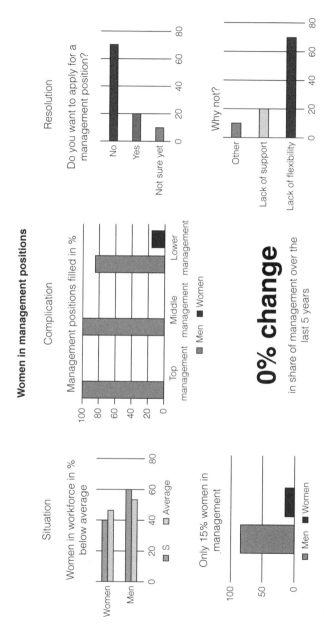

Figure 8.5 Example of a storified dashboard on diversity in management.

4. Involve: Engaging data audiences interactively

To involve others in the context of data means that you take your intended *audiences* into account when creating and presenting a chart. This can be done by giving your users simple ways of providing *feedback* to the chart and by enabling them to *deepen* their exploration by clicking on the chart.

In an interactive chart, you can involve your data users by letting them select areas of interest, zoom-in to more detail, explore different data aspects, filter out elements, customise the display, or connect it to new data.

In a live data presentation, you can involve the audience by letting them guess a result before showing it to them, or by asking the audience members what they find most striking in a particular chart. You can even go as far as asking them to put little sticky notes on a projected slide where they see further discussion needs or opportunities. This also works well virtually by using, for example, the Zoom annotation function that is active during on-screen presentations. Posting a downward arrow on a particular chart or section means that you want more detail about that data, while an arrow upwards would ask for the bigger picture or context of that data. A forward arrow would designate a discussion of the (action) implications of the data. A backwards arrow would signal the need to discuss the background of the data, such as the underlying sample. We call this approach to involve the audience through simple annotations 'navicons' as the placed icons help to navigate the dialogue about the data (Figure 8.6).

In all such presentations, remember to give your audience an *overview first*, and then *details-on-(their) demand*.

Broadly speaking, we are currently witnessing a shift in the analytics field away from simple one-way data presentation to more interactive data *facilitation* sessions – from merely presenting data to an audience to actively involving them in data dialogues. There is a myriad of free tools to support you in this endeavour, especially for virtual data talks. The most common software tools for this are miro.io or mural.co.

So: Be a (data) guide on the side, not a (statistics) sage on the stage.

Figure 8.6 Involving the audience in chart interpretation through navicons.
Source: ECB Meeting Lab

5. Give meaning: Eight ways to make data relatable

Data visualisation is all about making data *meaningful* for your audiences. There are at least eight ways in which you can assist this sense making process (this requires what is sometimes referred to as 'data screening'):

1. Linking data directly to possible *actions* or responses is one way to make it more meaningful (think bar chart on the left, recommended actions on the right).

2. Giving the chart an *action title* that expresses its so-what is another one.

3. Adding *self-explanatory labels* and axes descriptions to a chart helps to make it more meaningful even for hurried viewers.

4. Carefully adding *symbols* to a chart can help in its interpretation, for example a £, $ or € symbol for line charts with currency comparisons over time.

5. Explaining the reasons behind *outliers* or other strange data patterns (for example, through mouse-over comments).

6. Making data meaningful in a dashboard can be achieved by providing a *reference point* that shows whether a value is actually good or bad (above/below the target value).

7. You can also give meaning to numbers by showing them in their *development* over time.

8. Last but not least, you can make any number more relatable by *comparing* it to a phenomenon that the audience is *familiar* with,

163

for example by showing that the Amazon has lost more than ten million football fields of forest in a decade. This probably gives more meaning to that data than saying that there are 24,000 square miles of deforestation in the Amazon rainforest from 2010 to 2020. Another (more business-oriented) example is to illustrate the market capitalisation of Zoom Communications (the web-conferencing company) by showing that it is equivalent to the combined market capitalisation of seven major airlines.

Using one or several of these eight *interpretation aids* may require a bit of space or text, but the effort is well worth it to bring the data alive in the minds of the viewers.

So: **Giving data meaning requires data screening.**

6. No distortions: What to avoid in chart design

The general rule with this last principle is to steer clear of graphic formats that make data difficult to understand or easy to misinterpret (Figure 8.7). Such sub-optimal formats include pie/doughnut/arch charts – as they are perceptually inefficient and hard to compare, see the figure below – stacked bar and area charts (as they have moving baselines), or charts that mix units and have two different y axes in a single image. You also want to avoid line charts with many crossing lines, as they are especially hard to read due to the many intersections and overlap, and replace them with so-called small multiples.

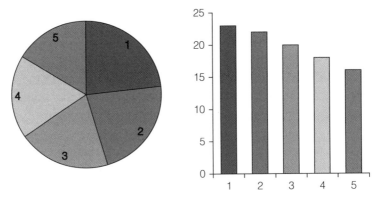

Figure 8.7 Pie versus bar chart: which communicates more clearly, accurately and quickly?

The no distortion rule not only applies to *how* you visualise data, but also to *which data* you visualise. Make sure you do not compare apples and pears or that you do not paint an incomplete picture by leaving crucial data out of the chart.

For an exhilarating compilation of chart examples that embrace such no-gos and fail in many different ways, check out https://viz.wtf/

So: Stay perceptually alert and leave the pie for dessert.

Data conversation (continued)

'The Survey Meeting':

It's the day of Arthur's presentation to the marketing staff. Luckily, this time he had a chance to discuss his charts with Phil before the meeting with the marketeers and simplified many of them in the process. But this time, it's a virtual, online session, which adds to Arthur's nervousness.

Arthur: Good morning folks, can you all hear me?

Steven: Loud and clear. We're ready for your chart junk Arthur (chuckles).

Arthur: Thanks Steven, I guess you heard about my last presentation. But let's get started. Have you ever wondered where we have the greatest up-sale potential in our business? Angie?

Angie: No clue, but dying to find out.

Arthur: You're about to. In this ranking chart you can see which of our offerings our clients know well, and what is still new to them. I highlighted the two items that are the least known in red. Here you guys need to get the word out about these two services as most customer segments are not aware of them.

Steven: Got it. Can you tell us a bit more about what channels the clients use or don't use to get info about our services?

Arthur: Yes, I've got that chart right here. As you can clearly see in this deviation chart, one of our key channels is

▶

widely under-utilised, and that is our online product and service catalogue. This trend line of the usage statistics of the catalogue shows that it has been popular at the launch, but since then very few clients use it. This means we must emphasise it more in our regular communication with clients. I added a little hand symbol to all chart sections where immediate action is needed, by the way.

Steven: Great idea, Arthur, and great charts, too. I didn't know youcouldtellsomuchwithsimplebarcharts.Consideryourself my virtual bar tender from now on.

Key take-aways

Let us recap our tour of data visualisation principles from a different angle. The guidelines discussed in this chapter focus on these crucial aspects of effective data charting, namely:

- the clean **style** of the chart (to declutter it)
- the fitting chart **format** for the data content (to emphasise its main message and guarantee that there are no distortions, detours, or misinterpretations)
- the creation and the delivery **process** (to involve others and tell a resonating story)
- the (decision) **context** of the chart through its title or caption and its labels, reference points, or symbols (to give meaning to the data).

This is all very useful, you may now say, but where is the secret that was promised at the start? Believe it or not, we can learn from a 19th-century poet, Matthew Arnold, when it comes to a good data visualisation style and his so-called 'secret of style'. He famously wrote:

'Have something to say and say it as clearly as you can. That is the only secret of style'.

So, make sure you visualise and communicate data that is *relevant* to your audience – or that you can make relevant to them. Do this as clearly as you possibly can and pre-check with a colleague if it really is clear to others. The DESIGN principles presented in this chapter will hopefully help you for that purpose.

Traps

Communication traps

To be aware of the possible risks inherent in data visualisation, go through the following checklist when you have prepared your charts:

Declutter   Emphasise   Storify   Involve Give meaning   No distortions

D.E.S.I.G.N. your Data – a simple Data Visualisation Checklist

A good chart is decluttered, emphasises its main message, tells a compelling story, involves the audience, gives a clear meaning and contains no distortions.

- **D**eclutter
  - Are borders, shades and 3D effects removed? ○
  - Is the accuracy level okay (no unnecessary details)? ○
  - Are the grid lines minimal and unobtrusive (as well as the labels)? ○
- **E**mphasise
  - Is the chart format supporting the chart's purpose? ○
  - Is more important information visually more dominant in the chart? ○
- **S**torify
  - Is the so-what of the data clear? ○
  - If there is more than one chart, are they in a logical sequence/arrangement? ○
  - Have you added a bit of drama or variety to the chart(s)? ○
- **I**nvolve
  - Have you sought feedback on the chart before communicating it widely? ○
  - Is there an easy feedback opportunity to the communicated chart? ○
  - Are there ways to interact with the chart if it is provided digitally? ○
- **G**ive meaning
  - Does the chart have a compelling title or caption? ○
  - Are there interpretation aids to guide viewers in making sense of the data? ○
  - Are the implications of the chart stated somewhere? ○
- **N**o distortions
  - Have you transformed all pie/donut/arc charts to bar charts? ○
  - Have you transformed a chart with many lines into several charts? ○
  - Have you eliminated sources of misinterpretation (such as cropped axes)? ○
  - Have you made sure that you did not leave out important data? ○

Further resources

You can find a very simple step-by-step example of how to declutter a chart at:

https://www.data-to-viz.com/caveat/declutter.html

You can find online examples of good guides to data visualisation at:

https://tinyurl.com/goodguidedataviz

https://medium.com/nightingale/style-guidelines-92ebe166addc

https://coolinfographics.com/dataviz-guides

http://visualizingrights.org/resources.html

https://visme.co/blog/data-visualization-best-practices/

https://killervisualstrategies.com/blog/three-rules-of-data-visualization.html

https://www.columnfivemedia.com/25-tips-to-upgrade-your-data-visualization-design

Notes

1. Have a look at the chart published in *The Economist* and spotted (and subsequently improved) on this site: https://www.vizsimply.com/blog/redesign-for-storytellingwithdata-part-1

2. At https://tinyurl.com/allviz

3. A great example of such 'scrollitelling' can be found at http://www.r2d3.us/visual-intro-to-machine-learning-part-1/

Chapter

9

The data storytelling canvas: Five magic ingredients for presenting data

What you'll learn

This chapter shows you how to use the key elements of storytelling for data presentations through a sequence of an intriguing beginning, an intense middle and a mobilising end. It highlights key success factors of data storytelling such as building common ground with the audience, triggering emotions or using your voice deliberately.

Data conversation

Sue: How did your presentation about the employee survey go this morning, Jeff?

Jeff: Well, I'm not sure. I did make it through the entire data set and all my slides, through all my calculations and all the survey's methodological issues in time. Some people had left early though and others were working on their computer, so a bit of mixed feelings here.

Sue: Do you think there is a chance that your data presentation was a bit monotonous?

Jeff: Mmm. Maybe I should not have shown all of it in our statistics software, but I wanted to keep it real, so I just showed them step-by-step how I imported and analysed the data. I almost ran out of time at the end, so I had to rush the actual results a bit.

Sue: I think you might want to radically reconsider your presentation approach.

As we have seen earlier, one of the best ways to talk about data is to visualise it. But simply turning heaps of data into charts will not do the trick (especially if you use pie charts, as we saw earlier). To make the work with data more seamless, you need to turn it into a *story* that is interesting, accessible and memorable (Figure 9.1). With the help of a simple tool, the data storytelling canvas, you can do just that and ease the burden on those who need to make sense of your data.

A story is an engaging narrative that has a clear, context-rich *beginning*, an intense *middle* and a satisfying *end* that leaves you with a sense of the 'so-what' of what has been told. Stories make you want to explore, dig deeper and truly understand what is going on. A good story is attention-grabbing and sustaining, intriguing and won't be forgotten easily. When it comes to decision-relevant data and its use in management, that is just what we are looking for.

So why should you care about stories? There simply is no better communication tool to inform, convince, engage or instruct others. We are all story-craving creatures, so why not use this formidable communication mode for one of the most complex forms of content – data?

For this purpose, we have created a simple tool – not only to deliver your data story visually, but also to prepare it in the visual working mode – the data storytelling canvas. It captures in a single framework everything you need to know about high-quality data storytelling.

You can use data storytelling and the following canvas whether you are a leader informing or persuading others with the help of data, or whether you are an analyst preparing dashboards, analytics and presentations.

The data storytelling canvas that we are about to present is a one-stop shop for any data communication opportunity. It will not only remind you of the key traits of a good data story, it will also serve as a *worksheet*. By completing it step-by-step, you can fast-prototype your data story, whether it's a presentation, a report, a dashboard or just a one-on-one briefing. This is particularly handy when you collaborate with others in preparing a data presentation, as the canvas serves as a sort of coordination device among you. Let's see how the canvas works and then how it can transform data into a lively story.

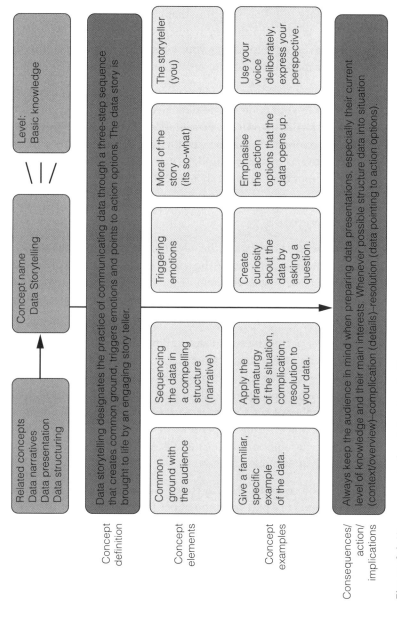

Figure 9.1 Key concepts for data storytelling.

The content of the figure:

Related concepts	Concept name	Level:
Data narratives	Data Storytelling	Basic knowledge
Data presentation		
Data structuring		

Concept definition: Data storytelling designates the practice of communicating data through a three-step sequence that creates common ground, triggers emotions and points to action options. The data story is brought to life by an engaging story teller.

Concept elements:
- Common ground with the audience
- Sequencing the data in a compelling structure (narrative)
- Triggering emotions
- Moral of the story (its so-what)
- The storyteller (you)

Concept examples:
- Give a familiar, specific example of the data.
- Apply the dramaturgy of the situation, complication, resolution to your data.
- Create curiosity about the data by asking a question.
- Emphasise the action options that the data opens up.
- Use your voice deliberately, express your perspective.

Consequences/action/implications: Always keep the audience in mind when preparing data presentations, especially their current level of knowledge and their main interests. Whenever possible structure data into situation (context/overview)–complication (details)–resolution (data pointing to action options).

The data storytelling canvas

As any canvas in the business context, this visual template offers you an easy-to-follow structure that you can fill in with your own content. It contains the key segments of a successful data story, whether you want to convey your latest customer survey findings, discuss a market study or present detailed risk analyses (Figure 9.2).

You can best work with the following canvas as an A3 print-out and then fill in your context and data elements into it. As Steve Jobs famously said, planning a presentation is best done in analogue, hands-on mode. This is also true for data storytelling. So, as counterintuitive as this may sound, switch off the computer when you prepare your data story. Grab a pen, and fill in the canvas.

The storytelling canvas consists of an upper *context* part, and a lower *story* part.

The upper part consists of the *subject* of the data story, the *audience* to whom you want to show the data, and your overall *goal* that you want to achieve with the help of the data. This part helps you to have a big picture view of your data storytelling effort. It ensures that your data story is audience-oriented and goal-driven.

The lower part is the actual storytelling tool that consists of three main parts labelled as 'Set the scene', 'Make your point' and the 'Conclusion'. Every good data story has these three elements in the sense of a beginning, a middle and an end. For each section, there are a number of key success factors, such as connecting with your audience and creating suspense with a big idea in the beginning, or triggering emotions in the middle, or providing a rewarding call to action at the end.

Before you complete these sections, however, you should expand on the audience part from the upper (context) part of the canvas: more specifically, you complete the *'Before'* and *'After'* sections by describing what the audience knows, believes, feels or wants *before* they have heard your story and *after*. This makes it clear what a difference your data presentation can make with the audience. What's their attitude about the topic before they have seen and heard your analyses, and what will it be (ideally) afterwards? Asking yourself this crucial question will help you focus your data story on the key parts that really matter (and decluttering your data story is often the most difficult part).

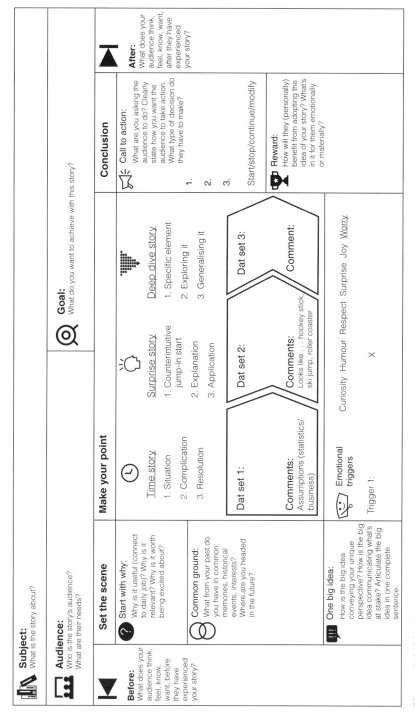

Figure 9.2 The data storytelling canvas.

Let us now look at the main part of the canvas in more detail.

Setting the scene: First impressions count, also in data storytelling. Resist the temptation to dive right into the data. Instead, first tell your audience *why* they should care about the data. Connect with your audience by relating the data to something that they already know (such as a recent event, the last presentation or a familiar challenge) so that you can build on a *common ground* when introducing new elements. It may also be useful to hint at the theme or *big idea* behind your presentation at this point and arouse your audience's interest in this way.

Making your point: When you then move to the meat on the bone, the actual data, it's useful to structure this main presentation into three acts that establish the *situation* (data that describes the status-quo), the *complication* (data that highlights the challenge or opportunity) and the *resolution* (if there is any) or a data-driven way forward that you propose. During these three acts one should not forget to make use of *emotional triggers* that help to sustain the attention of the audience or to make key data more memorable. Examples of such triggers are surprise elements of counterintuitive data, or estimation questions to the audience before you reveal the answer from the data. Think about how you can use your data to shock, to cause worry or pride, to intrigue or amuse. Above all else, however, you should make your point clear by avoiding jargon, explaining technical terms and providing accessible examples.

Conclusion: In closing your presentation you should reiterate the *call to action*, i.e., what you want your audience to do in light of the data that you have shown. This is particularly effective if you can tie this call to action to a *reward* that the audience can reap if they follow through with your advice. The reward is the positive outcome that will result (for the audience itself) from following your call to action.

In our experience, the *situation–complication–resolution* triad works for most data sets and presentations. However, you may also choose an alternative three-act structure at times.

Options for such formats are approach (a surprise story) or the *specific–explore–generalise* sequences (a deep dive story). In the first one, you grab everybody's attention by starting with a specific data set or insight that is likely to shock or surprise your audience. You then put this data set in a wider context, explain its background and finally show how to move forward given the evidence you have just presented. In the detail–generalise–suggest triad you begin with specific data and a small scope that is intriguing. You then show how this particular insight also resurfaced in other data (you generalise the insight). The last step is always the same in all structures: you suggest options for moving ahead.

In doing all this, your voice is actually an important storytelling tool to distinguish the different phases of your story. Let's see how our initial dialogue continued:

Data conversation (continued)

Sue: Have you used your voice to make your data presentation livelier or did you perhaps speak in a monotonous tone?

Jeff: I just told them everything I did and found. What do you mean using my voice?

Sue: I think you need to spice up your presentation tone, vary your voice more to keep people engaged to your data. There's an easy approach that I tried and that works. It involves using the metaphor of the four elements to distinguish your data segments vocally. It goes like this:

Earth voice: Use a solid, calm and deep voice to tell the audience about the data sources, the data quality, and the assumptions behind your analytics efforts in order to inspire trust and confidence in your audience.

Water voice: Use an 'easy listening' well flowing voice to explain your analysis approach and all methodological issues.

Fire voice: Use an energetic, strong, accentuated voice to announce the implications of the presented data and to articulate your call to action. This mobilises and motivates your audience to do something in light of the data.

Wind voice: For the ensuing question and answer session adapt your voice a bit to the dynamics of the conversation and the conversers themselves.

▶

Jeff:	Cool, I like it. It's simple, memorable and makes sense. I'm going to have to go outside my comfort zone though to put fire in my voice towards the end of my presentation for the call to action.
Sue:	Well, it should still feel authentic and natural to you. Don't overdo it, or it will sound fake.
Jeff (in a fiery voice):	You got it! That's what I'll do!

To see for yourself what this canvas can do to data presentation, let's have a look at a simple example: data about diversity. It will show you that even a dashboard can be storified.

A dashboard example

Let us say that you have gathered data about the current role of women in your organisation when it comes to their representation in management. You have conducted a survey on the female staff's eagerness to participate in management and, if lacking, why they might be hesitant to seek a management position. You now want to present this data in a compelling, easily understandable story to your top management. How do you go about this? In a first step, you visualise the key findings in charts, as you can see in the following illustration (Figure 9.3).

You may notice that the data for this particular organisation paints a bleak picture. Although women make up 60 per cent of the work force of this company, they have no representation in upper management, and only 15 per cent of the lower-management positions are filled by females. There is not a single woman in middle or upper management! What is worse, there has been no improvement whatsoever in this percentage of female representation over the last five years. A vast majority of the women do not even want to consider a career in management, as they feel there is a lack of flexibility in this organisation (when it comes to issues such has home office or flexible working hours).

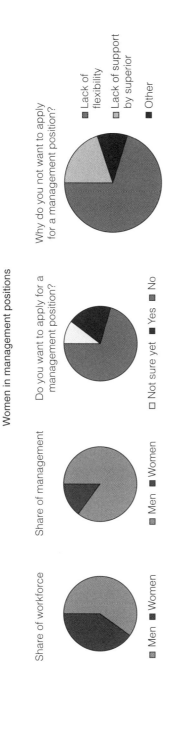

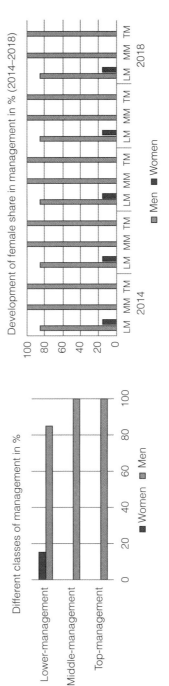

Figure 9.3 Non-storified dashboard version.

In a next step you can use the data storytelling canvas to structure your data in the situation–complication–resolution format (a time story). This, however, only after the context factors for the data presentation have been clarified. In this way, the data shown in Figure 9.3 are transformed into a storified version.

Based on this canvas, the initial data compilation (and subsequent dashboard screen) was then re-drawn to first convey the situation (that the majority of the workforce is female but their representation in management is low), and the complication that this representation is limited to lower management and that it has not changed in the last five years (Figure 9.4). The resolution that is then presented shows that one reason for this is that women do not want a position in management as it would entail a lack of flexibility. Women also perceive a lack of support from their leaders when it comes to pursuing a management career in this company. Ideally this call to action ('Be a better mentor, provide more flexibility!') is tied (at least verbally) to an explicit reward, such as 'this way we become more attractive as an employer, better as bosses, and more innovative as a company'.

You may have noticed that this dashboard version also contains an explanatory (action-oriented) *title* that is highlighting the 'morale' of the story, namely that there is a gap in management with regard to women, and that there is a clear call to action contained in the presented data (Figure 9.5). You probably noticed that the dashboard does not make any use of pie charts, as they are perceptually ineffective. Bar charts, and highlighted numbers communicate with more immediacy and ease.

In our research at the University of St. Gallen, we have found that people generally find this storified version of the dashboard more actionable, appealing and substantially clearer than the original version.

So, ask yourself these questions whenever you need to present data.

1. Which parts of this data are really relevant to achieve my objectives and effectively reach my audience (given their current level of knowledge and interest in the topic)?
2. How can I structure this data into a three-part sequence (i.e., situation–complication–resolution)?

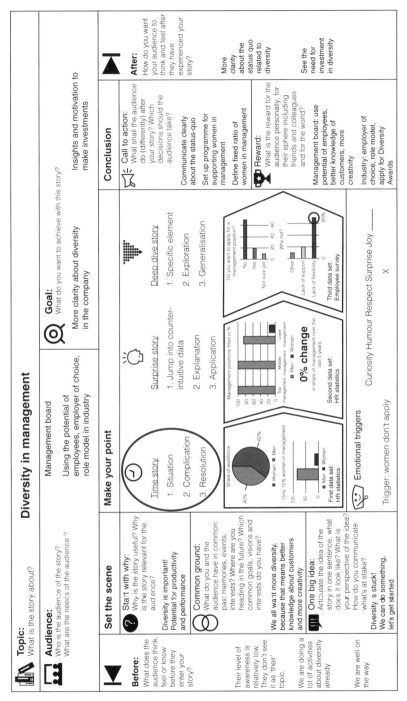

Topic:
What is the story about?

Audience:
Who is the audience of the story?
What are the needs of the audience?

Diversity in management

Management board
Using the potential of employees, employer of choice, role model in industry

Goal:
What do you want to achieve with this story?

More clarity about diversity in the company

Insights and motivation to make investments

Set the scene

Before:
What does the audience think, feel or know before they enter your story?

Their level of awareness is relatively low. They don't see it as 'their' topic.

We are doing a lot of activities about diversity already

We are well on the way

Start with why:
Why is the story useful? Why is the story relevant for the audience?

Diversity is important! Potential for productivity and performance

Common ground:
What do you and the audience have in common: past memories, events, interests? Where are you heading in the future? Which common goals, visions and interests do you have?

We all want more diversity, because that means better knowledge about customers and more creativity

One big idea:
Articulate the idea of the story in one sentence. what does it look like? What is your perspective of the idea? How do you communicate what's at stake?

Diversity's stuck! We can do something, let's get started

Make your point

Time story
1. Situation
2. Complication
3. Resolution

Share of workforce
40% / 60%
■ Women ■ Men

Only 15% women in management
100 / 50 / 0
■ Men ■ Women

First data set:
HR statistics

Surprise story
1. Jump into counter-intuitive data
2. Explanation
3. Application

Management positions filled in %
100 80 60 40 20 0
Top management / Middle management / Lower management
■ Men ■ Women

0% change
in share of management over the last 5 years

Second data set:
HR statistics

Deep dive story
1. Specific element
2. Exploration
3. Generalisation

Do you want to apply for a management position?
No / Yes / Not sure yet / Other
Why not?
0 20 40 60
Lack of support
Lack of flexibility — 80%

Third data set:
Employee survey

Emotional triggers

Trigger: women don't apply

Curiosity Humour Respect Surprise Joy
X

Conclusion

Call to action:
What shall the audience do (differently) after your story? Which decisions should the audience take?

Communicate clearly about the status-quo

Set up programme for supporting women in management

Define fixed ratio of women in management

Reward:
What is the reward for the audience personally, for their sphere including friends and colleagues and for the world?

Management board: use potential of employees, better knowledge of customers, more creativity

Industry: employer of choice, role model, apply for Diversity Awards

After:
How do you want your audience to think and feel after they have experienced your story?

More clarity about the status quo related to diversity

See the need for investment in diversity

Figure 9.4 The filled in canvas for the diversity example.

181

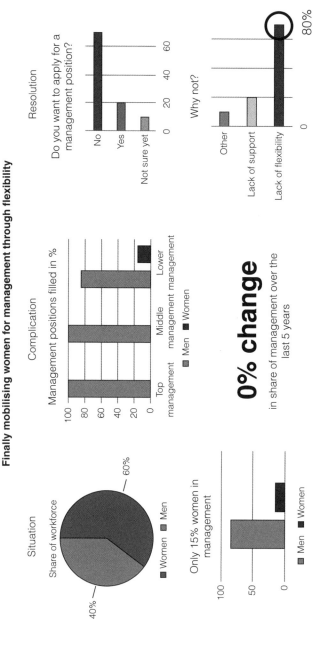

Figure 9.5 The storified data dashboard.

3. How can I start the data presentation with something that the audience already knows to establish common ground while also conveying a glimpse at a big idea that triggers their interest?

4. How can I surprise, intrigue, suspense, shock or amuse to make the data delivery more entertaining and memorable?

5. How can I conclude my story with a clear call to action and rewards (steps the audience can and wants to take in light of the data)?

To better remember the main ingredients of good data storytelling even when you're not using the above canvas, here is a memorable recap of the main ingredients of a good data story.

1. **Common ground: start with data examples that the audience knows and cares about**. Any good story lets the viewer or reader identify (to some degree) with the hero early on – think of Shrek (at the beginning of the movie with the same name) in the comfort of his own bubble bath. It creates a context where we can *relate* to the presented situation and see its *intrigue* and relevance to us. In a recent data presentation about expense analytics, a data scientist first talked to us about our phone bills and flight tickets before going into the metrics employed in his cost accounting. This helped everyone get what he was talking about.

   A good data story, consequently, does not start with abstract concepts or methodological issues, but with a concrete example of the data that the audience already knows and can relate to. A good data story best begins by showing the audience *why* this data matters (for them) and what the audience (most likely) already understands about this data (very briefly).

2. **Dramaturgy: structure your data into situation–complication–resolution**. A story is first and foremost a narrative, a plot, a sequence of events. This sequence is generally made up of three chapters: a first one to set the scene or explain the *situation*, a second one that introduces the hero's challenge or *complication* and a final one where this challenge is mastered and where we learn a lesson for the future (*resolution*).

   This threefold story structure can be applied to most data contexts by first showing data about the overall situation (of a market, customer base or business process), and then revealing the challenges or complications behind this by showing data in greater detail or for various aspects (for example, through drill-down functions in a dashboard).

In a final step, you should show the data that points towards solutions or next steps; data that highlights opportunities for improvements or changes.

3. **Emotional triggers: make your data engaging and emotionally meaningful.** No story can engage an audience without triggering emotions. There are plenty of ways in which you can trigger emotions with your data. You may want to stimulate curiosity (i.e., first raise a question, then provide data to answer it), shock (i.e., by showing counterintuitive data early on), intrigue (i.e., how will this trend continue?), remorse or even envy (i.e., regarding benchmarks or competitors' achievements).

So, think about what could be an emotion-triggering moment in your data presentation. Consider the surprise element in a new dashboard, such as showing unexpected but revealing reasons behind outliers when moving your mouse over them. Or start your market report by shocking (and intriguing) the reader with the most counterintuitive data patterns (and the fact that there is a simple explanation for them later on in the report).

4. **So-what: give a moral of the story that leads to a call to action.** A great story moves us to change our views, rethink our assumptions or even take action. A worthwhile story typically contains a moral (either implicitly or explicitly) that goes beyond the story per se and lets the readers or viewers derive consequences from it for themselves.

So, ideally your data story makes this moral or call to action explicit and ties it to a tangible reward (i.e., how the change will benefit the audience) to boost the motivation to take action.

A great way to *end* a data story is thus to give directions of where the data points to, in terms of action options, decision alternatives, or possible improvements. This is straightforward in a presentation or report, but a bit trickier in a dashboard. Nonetheless, some companies, such as reinsurance giant Swiss Re, have begun adding decision options or action implications to some of their dashboards.

5. **You are part of the story: give the data your perspective and tone of voice.** The last element of a good data story concerns

the narrator – you. Nobody wants to see a lifeless robot present data or read a text or dashboard that is style-wise (also concerning layout and graphics) boring, impersonal, and hence unappealing.

By now, we all suffer from Zoom fatigue, PowerPoint poisoning, and dashboard dementia, and thus personal style, the human element, is a breath of fresh air for any data story.

So put some of yourself in the story mix by (for example) emphasising data that you find personally particularly relevant or surprising, or by adding an element of individual *style* and tone to your presentation, dashboard, or report. Relate new data to other data that you have analysed before and put it in perspective this way. By doing this, you will enhance your audience's confidence in you and in the presented data.

Key take-aways

- Always have your audience and their level of knowledge and interest in mind when presenting data.
- Make your data interesting by scoping it, by making it accessible and by structuring it in a narrative (situation–complication–resolution).
- Put some energy in your data presentations, nothing is as contagious as enthusiasm. Vary your voice and end with a call to action.

 ## Traps

- Don't overuse emotions and use them only when they are appropriate. Be careful with humour or provocation. The safest emotions to use are curiosity and pride (when the data shows the team's achievements for example).
- Don't visualise all your data in charts. It's okay sometimes to just show a single number to emphasise its importance.
- Be careful when making recommendations derived from your data. Clarify upfront if this is really expected from the audience.

Further resources

Google's approach to data storytelling:

https://www.thinkwithgoogle.com/marketing-strategies/data-and-measurement/tell-meaningful-stories-with-data/

The English newspaper *The Guardian* has advice on data storytelling through journalistic examples:

https://www.theguardian.com/data

A useful blog on the topic:

http://www.storytellingwithdata.com

Chapter

10

Working with analytics software in front of others

What you'll learn

In this concise chapter you will learn what to watch out for when you guide people through data using a computer and a projector or in screen sharing mode online. We call these potential data presentation risks 'demo demons' that you better steer clear of.

Data conversation

Thomas: Jeff will now show us the new business dashboard that all of our sales staff can use to have a quick overview on what is going on in the market. Jeff, please go ahead.

Jeff: Thank you Thomas. Let me bring up the main starting screen. You can't really see it here, but down here you can actually customise your start screen. This was a really tough feature to implement by the way. Maybe I'll show you later how to adapt colours and fonts and different sizes. You can also modify how you want numbers to show down here.

Thomas: Jeff could you just show us the main features of the analytics dashboard?

Jeff: Um, sure. So, we have a markets data view and an internal data view with corresponding data about our different regions and our internal activities. What's really neat here is that you can change your data aggregation

▶

---

level using this slider, or this one, or you can also define those features in the settings page. Let me quickly go to that. I just saved the new settings and I'm back in the main menu. Wait, no, in the first submenu. But if I click here or drag it over here, then I can have my original view restored.

Thomas: Woah, that was a bit fast there. Can you show us what a typical user would do with the dashboard, say Monday Morning?

Jeff: Okay. Well I don't know what your job involves, but let's say you want to know how you rank compared to other sales staff. So watch how I do this in just six steps (quickly moves his mouse around and clicks on five different commands and menu items). Tada, that was cool, right?

Thomas: Yes, unfortunately I didn't get how you did that.

Jeff: You gotta know the software, I guess (smiles proudly).

Karen: Could I compare my performance to that of my most similar peers?

Jeff: I just did that before, didn't you see? I selected 'rank by similarity', duh!

Thomas: Okay, well, thanks Jeff. We look forward to using the dashboard. Perhaps we will include a user experience in our future town hall meeting.

Few things pain us more than having to endure a badly conducted software demonstration in a presentation or training. It's such a shame when there is a great piece of analytics software that is ill-explained or badly used.

Despite the importance of such software-based analytics presentations, we see this type of communication go wrong all the time – and it's not because the software crashes (Figure 10.1).

Having screened dozens of articles, posts and videos on how to 'demo software', we found that a lot of the advice out there is not really helpful, as it is either too obvious ('prepare well and keep the audience in mind'), or not specific enough ('use your time wisely').

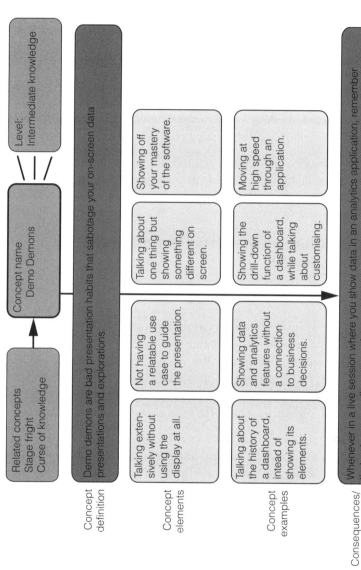

Related concepts
Stage fright
Curse of knowledge

Concept name
Demo Demons

Level:
Intermediate knowledge

Concept
definition

Demo demons are bad presentation habits that sabotage your on-screen data presentations and explorations.

Concept
elements

Talking extensively without using the display at all.

Not having a relatable use case to guide the presentation.

Talking about one thing but showing something different on screen.

Showing off your mastery of the software.

Concept
examples

Talking about the history of a dashboard, intead of showing its elements.

Showing data and analytics features without a connection to business decisions.

Showing the drill-down function of a dashboard, while talking about customising.

Moving at high speed through an application.

Consequences/
action/
implications

Whenever in a live session where you show data in an analytics application, remember that not every audience member regularly uses that application. Slow down. Align what you show and what you talk about and have a compelling user scenario in mind throughout your presentation

Figure 10.1 The concept of demo demons.

So, in this short chapter, we would like to share what we've learned about highly effective software demonstration practices and what the most common *soft*ware presentation errors are that you need to avoid when showing software to others.

This is important advice for anyone demoing or explaining software, whether as part of a presentation, in a venture pitch, during a one-on-one session, in team training, or during an e-learning module. We believe that our suggestions are also relevant for data scientists and analytics professionals who use interactive software in their collaboration with decision makers (for example, when explaining dashboards to managers).

Let's start with an overview of the typical 'demo demons', and then see how we can get rid of them to deliver outstanding software demos.

Demo demons: How software and analytics presentations fail

I (Martin) am generally a big fan of software, whether it's the latest version of a data visualisation package or the first release of a start-up's next killer app. But as most people, I get frustrated when I don't understand what is being shown. When software is shown on a projector, screen or online, it is crucial to guide the viewers carefully and make the demonstration an informative and *enjoyable* experience. Many presenters unknowingly sabotage this experience by committing one of the following demo disasters.

1. They start up the software (and thus create an immediate curiosity to see what it can do) and then continue talking for minutes *without any kind of screen action*. This creates impatience and irritation.

2. But also the opposite is not good practice, i.e., when presenters start *clicking away* without telling us their *goal* or their user scenario first. A good software demo needs context and a clear scope (for example, a focus on new functionalities).

3. Some software presenters show us complex functionalities while at the same time *talking about other issues,* such as why that functionality was difficult to implement. This makes it harder for the audience to focus on the software itself and understand what is

going on on-screen. Good software presenters *synchronise* tightly what they show and what they say.

4. Another bad habit of presenters is that they don't show us the *effect* of pressing a certain button or choosing an item. They simply assume we can see everything that is shown and notice even subtle changes.

5. Sometimes the demo folks want to impress us with their mastery of an application by being particularly *fast* in the execution of commands. The downside is of course that we can't follow what is happening. Pacing the demonstration adequately (including pausing or repeating a complex step) is thus a key success factor of any software demo.

6. Although it's easy to do, many presenters still don't visually emphasise the mouse pointer and *don't zoom into* the application to help us focus and see what they are doing (easy tools for this exist, see the next section).

Why do these mishaps occur? The short answer lies in a cognitive bias called the *curse of knowledge*. Once you have used an application for a while and understand it well, you become bad at explaining it to others. You simply have forgotten how complex the software is and assume it's simple for anyone else too. When you then demo it, you forget that many things are not as clear to others as they are – now – to you.

This is why we need to remind ourselves of essential presentation practices when it comes to using software in front of others. I summarise these essential practices in the next section.

Demo by design: Going from *what?* to *wow!*

How can you make sure that your audience not only understands what you're doing on the screen, but is actually enjoying it? Next to using your *voice* deliberately (avoid monotony) and spicing up your demo with a bit of *humour* and *personal touch*, the following *good practices* need to be kept in mind on every demo occasion:

1. Pick an example, data set, or user goal that the audience is *familiar* with and *cares about*. For example, in demonstrating a new data visualisation tool, use data about popular movies and show how they differ.

2. Build on what the audience is likely to know or understand already about the software's functionalities (emphasise the so-called *common ground*). You could relate new or crucial functionalities to famous user interface elements, for example those known from Windows or the Office suite.

3. To engage the audience, make sure that you have an early *'wow!' moment* in your demo that shows off what the software can do and what sets it apart from other applications. You have to make people aware of *unique features* and show your *enthusiasm* about them, as Steve Jobs famously did when first demoing the iPad over a decade ago (see the link at the end of this chapter).

4. Remember that an application's terminology is not self-explanatory. Make sure you define or *explain important terms* (beware of the curse of knowledge).

5. Keep your verbal explanations strictly *synchronised* with what is happening on the screen. Try not to refer to elements that the audience cannot see at that point in time.

6. Make sure you *zoom-in* to enable everyone to see what you're doing. *Highlighting* and marking may make important areas in the software even more salient. Zoomit.exe is a free and versatile tool for both zooming and highlighting.

If you remember these success factors and *adapt* your demo to the respective presentation setting, then your next software show will be a breeze – except of course, if the application crashes. But for this demo demon, you can always rely on good old backup slides with screenshots.

Data conversation (continued)

Thomas: As mentioned in our last meeting we now have a moment to highlight our sales dashboard use. Sebastian is an avid user of the application and will talk us through his use of it.

Sebastian: Thanks Thomas. Like many of you, I usually review my last month at the beginning of a new one. How would

---

the new dashboard help me there? First, I select the month I'm interested in. See how I pick the month on the top right-hand corner? That gives me the month in overview, but I still need to pick my region. I can do that here on the side. What you see now is all of April for my region. To see the sales events that go with these figures, I click on the plus-button underneath the axis now. Let me show you that again slowly. Any questions so far?

Ely: What happens if there have been too many events to fit in that space?

Sebastian: Great question, thank you. In that case, there is an expand button, the blue arrow right here (he zooms into the screen) at the end of the list of events that fit. Clicking on it reveals all the events. See, how it expands now. Does that make sense?

Ely: Totally, thank you!

Key take-aways

- Pick a compelling use case that the audience can relate to.
- Connect with the audience by connecting the data to their jobs and interests.
- Tell the audience what they are seeing.
- Zoom-in to make relevant details visible.

 ## Traps

Possible risks in on-screen data shows are:

- Frustrating or losing the audience early on.
- Boring the audience.
- Technical break-down, pauses, interruptions (thus: have backup slides).

Further resources

For a particularly memorable demo demon see:

https://tinyurl.com/demodemons

Further demo demons can be found at:

https://tinyurl.com/furtherdemodemons

To see Steve Jobs give the first iPad demo ever:

https://www.youtube.com/watch?v=OBhYxj2SvRI

Chapter

Delivering bad news with data: How to turn frustration into motivation

What you'll learn

This chapter shows what to do when data means bad news and why data can be a catalyst for improvement and progress. We offer practical communication strategies to convey bad data-based news so that you can avoid confusion, overcome resistance and turn frustration into motivation.

Data conversation

Alex looked at the report and instantly knew that it was bad news, very bad news. His team compiled an operations report and had discovered that there had been a continuously high reject rate in the production of an engine part. Alex knew that he had to inform the Executive Board including his boss, the Head of Operations, about this worrisome result. As he thought about how to present the findings, his hands became sweaty. Alex was a smart guy, with lots of experience in operations management. However, he had never considered himself a well-versed communicator and he often struggled to find the right words. At his last job, they had even told him that he had a 'special talent' to put things in an unintentionally rude and offensive manner. That had really struck him because he had never intended to be harsh to others or shame them with data. It was just that he had difficulties in communicating appropriately when delivering data-based insights.

▶

As he sat there, staring at the wall of his office, he wondered how to deliver unpleasant data-based news, especially when it means criticising your own boss? Alex remembered a recommendation that he had recently read, saying that one should communicate in an authentic way. And this was exactly what he wanted to do. He asked his team to conduct further analyses on the dataset, then compiled a short PowerPoint presentation and went into the meeting without much further preparation.

'Listen, I have to show you something', Alex began. 'My team found that we have continuous problems with the production of this engine part. For several weeks, there has been an unprecedented reject rate such that we have been wasting between 20% and 30% of the raw materials', he continued. Alex then added: 'We had a closer look at the data and noticed that the problems began after Matthew started running the operations unit. Moreover, the data reveal that most waste has been produced by Adriana's and Lorenzo's teams. Overall, the production needs to step up and do a better job.'

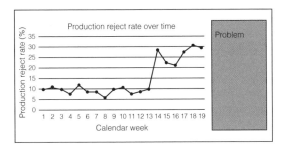

Slides from Alex's presentation.

Matthew, the Head of Operations, could not sit still anymore: 'This analysis is crap and misleading. The high reject rate is simply due to the fact that we changed one of our suppliers and that we realised too late that the product quality does not meet our standards. This has absolutely nothing to do with me nor with Adriana's or Lorenzo's teams. If this is all you have to say, consider this meeting over'.

Alex stood there, looking puzzled. Why had Matthew reacted so thin-skinned? To better understand what happened, Alex decided to talk about this incident with his colleague, Dean. After hearing what had occurred, Dean shook his head and said: 'Oh, boy, that was awkward. It is pretty obvious why Matthew became so furious'. Dean took a chair, sat down, and started to explain what went wrong . . .

After collecting and analysing data, you may have to present the results and conclusions to your colleagues and to your boss. But what do you do when you have bad news? Most people find it difficult to deliver bad news and thus avoid it as much as possible. This is intuitive and understandable because, generally, we do not like raining on other's parade or being killjoys. Bad data-based news are any insights that are based on data and that are regarded as unpleasant or undesirable and that come with adverse consequences (see Figure 11.1). And what different kinds of bad data-based news are there? There are at least three common types of bad news from data: negative trends, goal failure and insufficient competitiveness.

Negative trends refer to all kinds of undesired or disadvantageous developments. Examples of negative trends include steady drops in satisfaction among your employees or decreasing demand for your products. **Goal failure** means that you failed to achieve your set objectives. For instance, you may have provided medical supplies to 5,000 refugees instead of 15,000 or you may have acquired 100 new clients instead of 500. **Insufficient competitiveness** occurs when you are lagging behind compared to others or when you are doing comparatively less well. An example is when your

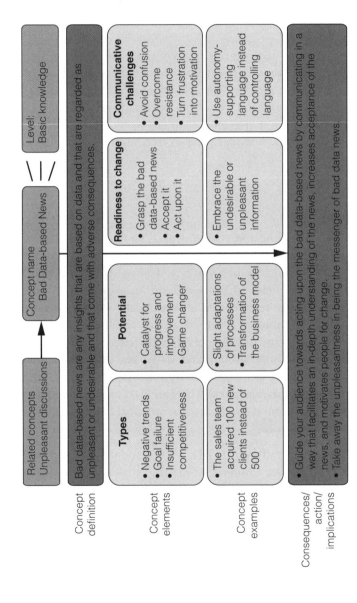

Figure 11.1 Key aspects of delivering bad news with data.

app is downloaded and used less frequently than the ones of your competitors.

Although **bad data-based news** is something from which we might intuitively shy away, there is a great potential to it. When communicated in a clever and compelling way, bad data news can be a (positive!) game changer. Bad news means that things have to change. Such change can range from slight adaptations to fundamental transformations – from modifying existing processes to restructuring the entire business model. Change is a process. It is something that evolves. Decades of research on behaviour change have shown that people have to move through certain stages before they are ready to alter the status quo (Bünzli and Eppler, 2019; Prochaska et al., 2008; Prochaska and DiClemente, 1982). Guiding people through these stages requires resonating and well-planned communication. We will show you how to successfully lead difficult data dialogues for the better. So, don't be afraid of delivering bad news when it's backed by data. Harness its potential for improvement (Figure 11.2).

Let's start with the three fundamental stages in people's readiness to seize the potential of bad data-based news. The first stage, the **comprehension** stage, is about understanding the data and its negative implications. People need to see the problem, its root causes and the resulting implications crystal clear. They can only move on

	Comprehension	Acceptance	Motivation
Audience perspective: Stages	Get the bad data-based news: fully grasp what the data mean.	Accept the bad data-based news: embrace the undesirable or unpleasant information that the data reveal.	Act upon the bad data-based news: be willing to use the insights for improvement and progress.
Messenger perspective: Goals:	Help your audience understand the problem and its causes.	Increase acceptance of your findings.	Motivate your audience to use the findings to make improvements.

Figure 11.2 Three fundamental stages of readiness to seize the potential of bad data news.

to the next stage if they thoroughly understand what kinds of data were collected, how the data were analysed and what the negative or worrisome findings are that derive from these data.

The second stage, the **acceptance** stage, is about embracing the undesirable or unpleasant information that the data reveal. People have to accept what they have learned from the data analysis. The key is to make them understand that the situation is serious, but that the findings do not represent a personal threat. When people incorporate the need for change, they can progress to the next stage.

The third stage, the **motivation** stage, is about the willingness to act upon the data. The audience has to be motivated to use the bad news to generate new ideas and come up with improvements.

Every stage is associated with particular challenges that can be addressed and overcome with clever data communication strategies. The biggest threat in the comprehension stage is **confusion** (Table 11.1). Your communication efforts should be aimed at clarifying your data sources, analytical procedures and findings. Thus, take your audience by the hand and guide them through the process of how you got to your conclusions. Elucidate where your data came from, how you proceeded with the analysis and elaborate on what the results mean (remember that data do not speak for themselves, they need to be interpreted and contextualised).

When delivering bad news, presenters sometimes rush right into the unpleasant findings before properly building their credibility (and the needed context). This immediate deep dive could overwhelm the audience. Similarly, speak in plain language and avoid data or statistics jargon or acronyms as much as possible (as this may aggravate people's resistance to the data even further). When people feel that you are speaking to them in riddles, they will not get the big picture of the bad news and fail to fully understand what you mean. Lastly, get to the point and be transparent about the extent and the severity of the bad news. This may be easier said than done because it involves telling your team or your boss straight away that things did not turn out as expected. It involves offering evidence in numbers and statistics that clearly demonstrate

Table 11.1 Key communicative challenge to the comprehension stage.

Stage	Comprehension: Get the bad data news	
Key challenge	**Confusion**	
Communication strategy	**Do**	**Don't**
Detail how you got to your findings and give an explanation or justification for your results instead of just confronting people with the outcome of your analysis.	'Our annual employee survey shows that our employees are less satisfied with their job than last year. 200 employees were randomly selected to take part in the survey. For the data analysis, we calculated the mean satisfaction. It showed that, on average, our employees are less satisfied with their job than last year. Their average satisfaction is 4.5 out of 10. Last year it was 6.6 out of 10. Moreover, the ratings are quite consistent as you can tell from the small spread of the data'.	'Our annual employee survey shows that the average satisfaction is 4.5 out of 10. Last year it was 6.6 out of 10'.
Speak in plain language instead of using data/statistics jargon or acronyms.	'Our data suggest a strong inverse relationship between the number of purchases in our web shop and the number of purchases in our flagship store. Specifically, the analysis revealed a correlation coefficient of –0.8. That means, as the number of products our clients buy in our web shop increases, the number of purchases in our flagship store decreases'.	'The analysis revealed a correlation coefficient of –0.8 between the number of purchases in our web shop and the number of purchases in our flagship store'
Get to the point and be transparent instead of sugar-coating things.	'The sales went down by 40% this year compared to last year'.	'The sales were a bit below expectations this year'.

what is going wrong. Be aware that you do not resolve the problem by sugar-coating bad news (or tuning your findings to the expectations of the audience). It gives your audience a wrong impression and may lead them to not take the problem seriously enough.

You may have successfully brought your audience to understand the bad data-based news. However, that does not necessarily mean that they will accept it. In fact, we often see that people exhibit severe resistance to bad news. When talking about resistance, we are referring to a key challenge of the acceptance stage. Overcoming resistance means getting people to accept the bad news that your data reveals.

There are several communication strategies that have shown to be beneficial to this endeavour (Table 11.2). First of all, pay attention to the way you frame your data interpretation. Often, we can express *the same thing* using a loss-framed perspective or a gain-framed perspective. A loss-framed perspective puts emphasis on negative aspects or disadvantages (e.g., '3 out of 10 customers would not recommend our product'), whereas a gain-framed perspective emphasises positive aspects or advantages ('7 out of 10 customers would recommend our product'). Even when conveying bad news, try to weave in some gain-framed elements. The reason is simple: too much negativity is daunting and might give your audience the impression that there is no hope for improvement. This might create perceptions of not having an option and, as a result, might evoke resistance (Cho and Sands, 2011). Framing some findings in gain terms helps people see a silver lining on the horizon and makes it easier to accept that some things are not yet where they are supposed to be.

Second, mind your language when formulating recommendations. You spent a lot of time squeezing out insights from your data. It is legitimate that you are convinced of what you did and that you want to make sure everyone gets the implications that your data bear. However, as often in life, it is the tone that makes the music. Several decades of research have shown that controlling language triggers resistance, whereas autonomy-supporting language attenuates it (Rosenberg and Siegel, 2018; Steindl *et al.*, 2015). What is meant by that? Controlling language includes terms such as

Table 11.2 Key communicative challenge to the acceptance stage.

Stage	Acceptance: Accept the bad data news	
Key challenge	**Resistance**	
Communication strategy	**Do**	**Don't**
Use gain-framing instead of loss-framing when interpreting your data.	'7 out of 10 customers would recommend our product'	'3 out of 10 customers would not recommend our product'
Use autonomy-supporting language instead of assertive language when deriving recommendations from your data.	'You may want to consider layoffs'; 'It might be time to revise the strategy'.	'You should lay off people'. 'You must revise the strategy now'.
Be calm and professional instead of joking.	'This result is concerning and shows that the drug did not work as expected. I therefore suggest that we . . . '	'The drug did not work as expected. By the way – do you know why ants don't get sick? Because they have anty-bodies'.
Make clear that you are only the messenger and do not take the blame for things that are outside of your responsibility.	'John, please consider that I am only the messenger. I did the analysis on the data and compiled the charts'.	'John, I am so sorry for these results. I feel terrible about it'.
Express empathy and give recognition instead of only criticising people.	'I understand that these results may be frustrating. However, you did a great job in projects X and Y'.	'The numbers are thoroughly bad. You have to step up your game'.

'should', 'must', 'ought'. Autonomy-supporting language includes terms such as 'consider', 'may', 'might', 'could'. Controlling language gives people the impression that they are being told what to do and that they cannot choose. This is counterproductive because it encourages (overt) rejection of your recommendation. This particularly applies to situations in which you confront people with bad news. No one likes to hear that they failed to meet the goals or that their project performed below expectations. This is even worse when you tell them in a dogmatic way how they should do things. Therefore, use autonomy-supporting language whenever you are presenting the implications of your data.

Third, stay calm and professional. Most people feel uncomfortable when delivering bad news. To hide their unease, they sometimes make jokes about the things that went wrong. Using humour in such situations, however, often backfires. Imagine that someone tells you (in front of others) that the sales of your product crashed. The last thing you would want is that this person makes jokes about your problem. You would likely find it offensive, rude and unemphatic. When feeling offended or attacked, people frequently engage in counter-arguing. They question the reliability or validity of the data, the data analysis, or even the competence of the presenter. This is bad – not only for the presenter but also for the quality of the data discussion. Counter-arguing for the sake of defending oneself (or one's ego) distracts attention from the actual problem and leads to unproductive and unsatisfying data discussions and eventually to bad decisions.

But what can you do if this does happen? Say, if someone questions what you did or what you know? Make clear that you are only the messenger and that you did not cause the problem (e.g., 'John please consider that I am only the messenger . . . '). You do not need to take the blame for things that are outside your responsibility. Nevertheless, be empathic and put yourself into the shoes of your audience. Being confronted with bad news can be overwhelming and can lead to people (occasionally) losing their composure. Think about how you would feel if you were given the same bad news. This might help you come up with the right words to calm down your counterpart and to reduce the emotions in the discussion. If someone is persistently criticising the data quality or the data analysis, it might be helpful to go back and give some details on your sampling and analysis again. To better prepare for criticism and counter-arguing, you may also want to write down a list with 'nasty questions' in advance of your presentation. Think of any kinds of tricky (or mean) questions that could be raised by the audience and develop answers to these questions. Common examples of nasty questions include: 'Why didn't you use approach X instead of Y to analyse the data?'

or 'To what extent is the data biased and how might this affect the results'?

You may have brought people to accept your findings. However, that does not mean that they are willing to act upon the bad news. This brings us right to the key challenge of the action stage: that is, **frustration**. Overcoming frustration means to motivate people to take action and to improve things. In the following, we have synthesised several communication strategies that are helpful to battle inertia (Table 11.3). When talking about the next steps, give a proactive outlook instead of an avoidance-oriented outlook. A proactive, approach-oriented outlook focuses on possible positive outcomes (e.g., 'Overall, adjusting our customer service will be key to retaining more customers'), whereas an avoidance-oriented outlook focuses on possible negative outcomes (e.g., 'Overall, being vigilant of the customer service will be key to not lose more

Table 11.3 Key communicative challenge to the motivation stage.

Stage	Motivation: Act upon the bad news:	
Key challenge	**Frustration**	
Communication strategy	**Do**	**Don't**
Provide an approach-oriented outlook (focusing on positive outcomes) instead of an avoidance-oriented outlook (focusing on negative outcomes).	'Overall, adjusting our customer service will be key to retaining more customers'.	'Overall, being vigilant of the customer service will be key to not lose more customers'.
End on an optimistic note instead of a pessimistic note.	'Although things did not turn out as we had hoped, let's take these insights as an opportunity to boost our business'.	'Things did not turn out as we had hoped. This is frustrating, but it is what it is'.
Give your audience the opportunity to ask questions and speak their minds instead of rushing out of the meeting.	'I would like to invite you to ask questions, share your ideas, and reflect upon these findings'.	'Okay, that's it. Thanks for your attention'.

Data conversation (continued)

Dean took a deep breath and described what went wrong when Alex had delivered the bad data news to the Executive Board.

'Look, not only is it unpleasant to be confronted with bad news, also it is uncomfortable being blamed for negative outcomes', he said. 'You mentioned that the increased reject rates had been occurring since Matthew was in the position as Head of Operations and that most had been produced by Adriana's and Lorenzo's teams. You put the blame on them personally and made them the culprits. They lost face in front of all the other members of the Executive Board', Dean argued. Alex frowned as he began to realise what he did. 'If people feel that they lose face, they feel the urge to defend themselves. And as they concentrate on restoring their reputation, they are not open to rational and objective discussions anymore', Dean added. 'I see the problem, but what should I have said instead? I can't sugarcoat the data', Alex said in a desperate tone.

Dean reflected for a moment and then responded: 'First of all, you should have been better prepared. It's not enough to only deliver the bad news. You have to dig deeper and try to squeeze the reasons for the undesirable outcomes out of the data. What led to these problems? And second, make more informed choices regarding the level of analysis. The more fine-grained your analysis, the easier it might be to link the results to specific teams or people. Thus, always ask yourself in advance, whether your data allow you to identify groups or individuals. And if so, evaluate whether this is necessary and whether it provides any value added. And third, when criticising others, give recognition of their previous work and mention which other factors may have negatively influenced their performance. People are generally motivated to do a good job and they are sad or frustrated when things do not turn out as expected. So, acknowledge their effort when delivering bad news and shed some light on the context of the data'.

'You're right about these aspects. I think I have to apologise to Matthew, Adriana and Lorenzo for not being fair. I definitely have to work on my data communication skills', Alex said.

customers'). An approach-oriented outlook sparks motivation and optimism because it emphasises what people can gain by adjusting things. If available, use further data to underline your claim. Show your audience, for instance, how other units at your organisation managed to turn around a negative trend, how long it took them, or what measures were taken. Similarly, end on an optimistic note when finishing your presentation. Keep in mind that there is something called the 'Recency Effect', a cognitive bias where people tend to remember the most recently presented information best.[1] This means that things that you say at the end of your presentation will be the ones that stick in people's minds. Thus, make sure that this is something positive and encouraging.

There is another powerful way to avoid frustration in your audience – something intuitive that is, however, often neglected: Give your audience the opportunity to ask questions, speak their minds and develop ideas. Overcoming frustration is not only a matter of preaching to the people and finding encouraging words, but also of giving them the space to become active and coming up with their *own* suggestions. Thus, allocate sufficient time for a Q&A session at the end or for an exchange of ideas.

Key take-aways

Most people feel stressed and uncomfortable when delivering bad news with data. However, this must not necessarily be the case as unpleasant data can be an important catalyst for improvement and progress. The art is to deliver such news in a way that the audience can understand the analysis, accepts its results, and feels motivated and empowered to take action. You may find the following questions helpful when preparing to deliver bad news with data.

1. What kind of bad news do your data reveal: negative trends, goal failure or insufficient competitiveness?

2. How do you ensure that your audience fully grasps the data? ➤ Avoid confusion (see page 205).

3. What can you do to increase acceptance of your findings? ➤ Avoid resistance (see page 207).

4. How do you motivate your audience to change things? ➤ Avoid frustration (see page 209).

 Traps

Communication traps

Table 11.4 Dos and don'ts of communicating bad news with data.

Dos	Don'ts
• Get to the point.	• Sugar-coat things.
• Speak in plain language.	• Use data/statistics jargon and acronyms.
• Detail how you got to your findings.	• Confront people only with the outcome of your analysis regardless of context.
• Use gain-framing.	• Use loss-framing.
• Use autonomy-supporting language.	• Use controlling, dogmatic language.
• Be calm and professional.	• Joke around.
• Tell people not to shoot the messenger.	• Take the blame and apologise for things outside your responsibility.
• Be empathetic and acknowledge people's effort.	• Fail to acknowledge other's feelings and their effort.
• Prepare a list of 'nasty questions'.	• Go unprepared and see how things turn out.
• Provide an approach-oriented outlook.	• Provide an avoidance-oriented outlook.
• End on an optimistic note.	• End on a pessimistic note.
• Give your audience time to speak their mind.	• Rush out of the meeting after your presentation and leave people alone with the bad news.

DON'T

> I can't believe it. You had one job and you failed. Just look at the data from the customer survey. The mean perceived user friendliness of our app is 3.5, whereas the mean perceived user friendliness of the competitor's app is 8.8. This difference is significant, as the p-value is below the 0.05-criterion. You must work harder and see how you can fix this. We can't afford offering bad products. That's it for now. We will meet again in a few days.

Example of how not to communicate bad news with data.

DO

> Despite our continuous efforts, the results of the latest customer survey are not in our favour. Our online trading app was outperformed by the competitor's app. Look at the differences in the average perceived user friendliness. The mean perceived user friendliness of our app is 3.5, whereas the mean perceived user friendliness of the competitor's app is 8.8. The very small p-value further suggests that this difference did not occur by chance. Thus, it might be time to come up with an 'emergency plan'. Let's take this result as a motivation to improve our app and to develop the leading online trading app on the market. I would like to use the remainder of the time to start collecting and discussing ideas. Any comments? Thoughts? Suggestions?

Example of how to communicate bad news with data.

Further resources

To learn more about how to deliver bad news see:

https://www.forbes.com/sites/forbescommunicationscouncil/2019/04/03/13-ways-to-get-better-at-delivering-bad-news/?sh=29c7087865f0

https://www.youtube.com/watch?v=s76bX5ujl_4

Note

1. https://dictionary.apa.org/recency-effect

Chapter

12

Handling data disagreements: Argue with and about data

What you'll learn

Being able to argue over data is an important analytics capability today, as data is not always clear-cut in terms of its quality, interpretation or application. You need to learn how to argue with and about data and have good fights over it to get the most value from it. This is what this chapter will instruct you to do. Companies such as the industry group Swiss Re or the Technical University of Sydney consider arguing with data and managing data disagreements key elements of data literacy. So let's get ready to rumble.

Data conversation

Setting: A meeting room in the upper floor of a large building complex. Participants: a corporate merger and acquisition task force consisting of bankers, lawyers and financial consultants. The mood: Tense.

Peter: So, looking at the performance data in review, it seems clear to me that we need to stop this acquisition project at this point. The candidate company looked good at first glance, but having carefully looked at its financial and commercial data, we believe it is best to stop the due diligence process and tell our counter party that the deal won't happen after all.

Ellen: Peter, that is not at all what the data says, who had you go through it, an intern, or the guys from the post office?

Peter: My team of analysts looked at all data points very carefully, including cost data, supplier data and historic

---

▶

sales and profitability data. What gives you the right to question our methods? Our track record is rock solid. So, anyhow, we concluded that the performance data from the last 5 years was mediocre at best and that we should not acquire this company.

Ellen: You should have looked at the more recent sales data and especially the trend data regarding customer spend. That's what you should have done.

Peter: We took that into account.

Ellen: If you had, you'd come to another conclusion, just run a regression and you'll see that customer spend drives profitability in the medium term. Steve, I suggest we have another team look at the performance data and I'm sure they will share my conclusion that the outlook of that company is extremely promising.

Steve: But Ellen, Peter's team did a thorough job analysing the data. Are you saying they don't know what they're doing?

Ellen: I don't know what they did, but the data does tell another story, believe me.

Steve: I trust Peter and his work, but I also heard that there are data quality issues when it comes to the company's sales forecasting data. So, here's what we will do. We'll set up a slightly longer meeting where Peter and his analysts will show us the key data, metrics and analyses that they have conducted. We'll take a deep dive to see how serious the performance gaps really are and what kind of outlook makes sense. Is Monday doable for that Peter?

Peter: I think so, yes.

Steve: Good. In the meantime, Ellen, you will have full access to Peter's analyses, and you can flag anything where you might disagree. We can then also discuss this next Monday.

In business, nobody likes a fight. Sometimes, however, you need to engage in controversial discussions surrounding data. Why? To shed different perspectives on the scope of data, its quality, its analysis, and interpretation, and ultimately its use. Only when you combine different perspectives in your data dialogues, can you be sure that you're using data well (Figure 12.1).

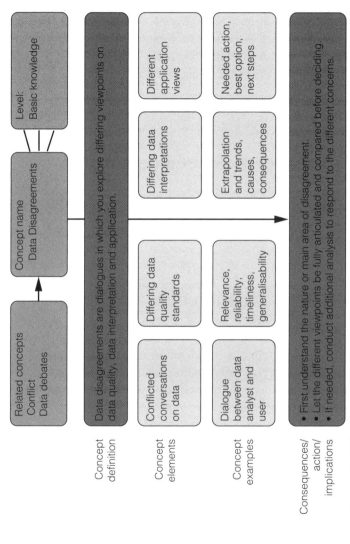

Figure 12.1 The concept of data disagreements.

219

The technical perspective of your data analysts, for example, should be combined with the manager's bigger picture and strategic outlook. Alternatively, different sector experts may have a healthy debate about their respective data and how it might be combined.

The bottom line is: if you want to get the full value from data, you should not shy away from dissensus around it, but embrace good fights. In such debates, the common goal should be to come to a higher level of understanding of the data and clearly see its potential, but also its shortcomings and limitations.

To do this, we present a simple four-step process for productive data dissensus.

A process for data-centred debates

So, how can you design a dialogue that leads to productive disagreement instead of an abrasive clash of viewpoints? Here's our four-step design approach.

1. Frame it right

Whenever discussing an issue, frame the disagreement positively by inviting more perspectives, experiences, options, or insights. Don't frame a controversial discussion as 'let the stronger argument win', but rather as 'let's have as many angles as could be useful on this data'. Label it as '360 degrees thinking' rather than 'a crossing of swords'. Learn from designers and artists: how you label something influences its perception and use. Part of the framing is also pinpointing the specific areas of disagreement about the discussed data. So, in other words: understand which type of disagreement is there or where the source of the disagreement lies, and where you may have consensus already. Are there different views regarding the data's quality, its interpretation, or how to apply it to the decision at hand? Answering this question early is crucial for more productive data dialogues. Also visualisation, our step 2, may help you clarify the issues with the data.

2. Visualise it right

By using instant polling tools such as Mentimeter.com (which also provides anonymity) or offline means such as dots and whiteboards, you can visualise the different viewpoints in a joint framework so that minority views surface and so that you can truly see the degree of consensus or dissensus about the discussed data. Figure 12.2 provides an example of such a dissensus visualisation where we can see that although the average view on data set 3 is positive (it's in the top right-hand corner), there are eight colleagues who have rated it as not very reliable (the left side of the grid). This visualised variety empowers them to speak up and share their reliability concerns with the others. Their sceptical votes may help to examine potential data deficiencies in dataset 3 or clarify their doubts. So, look beyond the average votes and examine the spread of opinions (represented by the individual small dots in the diagram).

You can also see in the diagram that four people are doubtful about the data set's applicability to the decision that needs to be taken. Again, encouraging them to speak up will help you assess the data better and recognise its limitations.

3. Discuss it right

Using the dissensus visualisation, direct criticism at the visualised issues and not at the people in the room. Separate the arguments from the person and discuss why minority views may have merit (irrespective of seniority). Spend more time on discussing data with high dissensus and a bit less time on areas where agreement

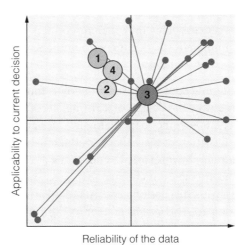

Figure 12.2 Dissenting views on data.

has already been reached. The following data discussion principles can help you in that endeavour.

1. *Questions first*: Don't feel shy about validating your understanding of the data before criticising it (also see Chapter 7 on analytics Q&A for this point). Ask for details regarding sampling, variable and data definitions, statistical procedures used etc.

2. *Constructive criticism*: Don't just criticise the data, but add suggestions on how to improve the data's reliability or applicability.

3. *Connect the dots*: Make sure, especially as a facilitator of data dialogues, that you relate the different views voiced about the data to each other and to possible action implications (such as data cleansing or additional data gathering activities). This last principle leads us to the final step in our process: consolidating the debate.

4. Consolidate it right

Discuss how the minority views could be incorporated in the team's (or your own) decision and combine the proposed arguments so that they lead to a richer, *joint* picture and ultimately to a more refined view on the data. In consolidating the views of your teammates, work with visualisations that signal that they are subject to revision and work in progress. Use flipchart drawings, whiteboards sketching and the like to invite others to refine the joint level of understanding by adding new considerations or modifying existing ones. Don't forget to capture the to do's that surfaced during this process. This may include refined data analyses, additional sampling efforts, dealing with outliers, or re-running certain statistical procedures.

Designing data dissensus properly is thus a crucial analytics task. It requires the design of a fitting *label* for a dissensus discussion (i.e., '360 degrees data dialogue'), designing a *visual representation* of the different views (such as the reliability–applicability matrix example above), as well as designing a conversation *process* around minority views or counter opinions. The last element for fruitful dissensus discussions consists of creating a fluid yet convergent design for the *documentation* of the results. This may include a graphic ranking of data issues from the most to the least controversial one (and the measures that should be taken).

⚠ **How to say it**

Avoiding confrontation and saving face

Criticising data and the underlying analytics is important, but you have to find the right way to do it. Good data debates are all about joint learning and improving together. To avoid hurting someone's professional pride in the process, try these ways outlined in Table 12.1 to soften your critique but still be crystal clear.

Table 12.1 How to avoid confrontation and save face.

Instead of saying this	Try this
You don't know what you are doing.	Which methods have you used and are you a 100 per cent sure they fit the data?
I don't trust your work.	Show me how you proceeded step-by-step when analysing this data.
I don't trust this data.	Can we be sure that this data is reliable? What gives you confidence in this data?
This data is irrelevant.	Are you sure that this is the right data to consult for this decision?
Your interpretation of this data is ludicrous.	Help me understand how you draw those conclusions from the data.
This makes no sense whatsoever.	I really need to understand what you have done in terms of analytics, so please go through this again step-by-step.
Do you even believe in what you're saying here?	Where are areas where you have less certainty when it comes to the data interpretation?

Data conversation (continued)

Steve: Thanks Peter for preparing the analysis presentation and Ellen for playing the devil's advocate. I'm glad that we can have this 360-degree view on the due diligence data today. Just a *few ground rules* before we get started. Our goal is not to see who is right, but to achieve a common understanding of the company's financial situation and outlook based on the data that we have been able to access. I want us to be constructive and argue about the data, not the people. Okay?

Ellen: For sure. Peter's team had a lot of data to go through and I saw that they did a very thorough job. I just see a few points differently that's all.

Steve: Good, we will get to those. Peter, can you focus on the last two years in sales of this company and what conclusions you drew from the data and how?

Peter: Gladly, yes.

Ellen: And show us the stats you ran on this too, please. You did run a regression, right?

Peter: Yes, after your suggestion, we did a regression and current customer spend seems to be a good predictor for future sales. Based on the recent customer spend data, the outlook is indeed more positive than one could think looking only at the past performance track record in terms of sales volume, and partly also profitability.

Ellen: You still seem sceptical though?

Peter: Yes, that is because our analysis of their cost accounting data revealed that they manage cost and suppliers badly. We've been able to collect benchmark data as well, and our candidate company finishes last in terms of cost efficiency. And the situation doesn't really seem to improve.

Ellen: Okay I admit I didn't run all the numbers regarding cost evolution. But we could help them in that, right? We

---

> could help them keep costs down and become more competitive.
>
> *Peter:* I guess we would be able to, yes. However, our own track record is not spotless. We are usually not in the top group when it comes to cost management. Because of this, our recommendation was to stop the due diligence at this point.
>
> *Steve:* So, sales wise the data warrants our optimism, but the cost development is of concern. Great that we have gotten to this joint understanding. I suggest we ask for an additional week to identify cost reduction potential. If this does not materialise within 5 days, we stop the whole exercise.

Discussing data often comes with differing points of view and thankfully so. We need to embrace disagreement about the relevance, reliability and scope of data in order to make high-quality evidence-based decisions. Otherwise we have an illusion of reliable data, and an illusion of consensus, where there really isn't. So don't shy away from grilling your analysts, but do so respecting the rules of constructive criticism, and by first making sure you really understand the data and the areas of disagreement.

Key take-aways

- Don't see data as a given, but understand that they are the result of human choices.
- Actively invite different perspectives about data when interpreting it. Ask questions such as: 'Is anyone sceptical about where this data has come from or how it's been analysed?'
- Give voice to sceptics, dissenters and contrarians or minority opinions and try to integrate their concerns into your data dialogues. Sometimes it's better to surface such potential dissenting opinions before an actual meeting in bilateral formats.

Traps

Communication traps

- Don't let criticism get personal and affect work relationships. Set ground rules for constructive criticism.
- Generally, beware of finger pointing and making data disagreements about culprits.
- Beware of a comprehensive data critique and pinpoint potential biases or data issues as specifically as possible.

Further resources

These are great articles on how to have better disagreements in general:

Edmondson, V.C. and Munchus, G. (2007) Managing the unwanted truth: A framework for dissent strategy. *Journal of Organizational Change Management*, 20(6), 747–760.

Garner, J.T. (2012) Making waves at work: Perceived effectiveness and appropriateness of organizational dissent messages. *Management Communication Quarterly*, 26(2), 224–240.

Leigh, P., Francesca, G. and Larrick, R. (2013) When power makes others speechless: The negative impact of leader power on team performance. *Academy of Management Journal*, 56(5), 1465–1486.

Mengis, J. and Eppler, M.J. (2006) Seeing versus arguing: The moderating role of collaborative visualization in team knowledge integration. *Journal of Universal Knowledge Management*, 1(3), 151–162.

Schulz-Hardt, S., Brodbeck, F.C., Mojzisch, A., Kerschreiter, R. and Frey, D. (2006) Group decision making in hidden profile situations: Dissent as a facilitator for decision quality. *Journal of Personality and Social Psychology*, 91(6), 1080–1093.

Chapter

13

What's next? Sustaining your data fluency

What you'll learn

In this concluding chapter we summarise the main contents of the book in the form of an ideal 'data converser' *profile* and their skills, attitudes and resources. The chapter highlights that it's not just important how you talk about data, but also to *whom* you're talking, and what their role is in the analytics field. We also point to emerging *trends* in analytics that you need to monitor – even as a generalist. This chapter also provides you with pointers to useful resources to keep your analytics skills current. Last but not least, we articulate a *way forward* in which you can now make the best use of what you have learned in this book and ensure your continued progress.

Congratulations! You have made it through the key concepts of statistics, analytics and data communication. You are now well equipped to talk competently, clearly and critically about data and analytics.

You have achieved a solid level of data fluency that boosts your employability and opens up many new options for your career or next ventures.

Being fluid in data is, however, not just a question of understanding or of skills. It is also dependent on your *attitude* and on the *resources* that you have available. Let's look at these three elements of *sustained* data fluency in more detail and with the help of a final dialogue. This will assist us in consolidating our learnings on how to talk about data and brings them to life.

Data conversation

Joana is a successful, 32-year-old, enthusiastic project manager, working for a mid-size service organisation. Her background is in marketing, but she has recently developed a keen interest in information technology and analytics.

She realises that her projects (and marketing in general) are ever more affected by data and its analysis. She enjoys learning and interacting with people and thus talks to a colleague of hers in the IT department. She wonders how she might develop her analytics skills and catches the colleague during a coffee break:

Joana: Gordon, I know you are super busy, but do you have a minute for me?

Gordon: Sure thing. What's on your mind Joana?

Joana: You know I've been working in marketing and project management for the last six years and I feel that my data skills are not where they should be. What's your advice for me? What does it take to be fluent in data and analytics?

Gordon: You won't like my answer, but I've found out the hard way that most of what we call data science today is actually statistics, with a bit of data management thrown in of course. But to talk about data, you first need to understand statistics.

Joana: Oh, I will have to revive that stuff from my university days then. And where do you think could somebody like me add value in the analytics realm?

Gordon: So many insights from analytics get lost in communication. That is why I believe the key skills are making data accessible, visualising data and handling data in group settings. I've seen that this often breaks down, especially among analysts and managers.

Joana: Got it. So I should focus on elements such as data storytelling right and ramping up my charting skills, right?

Gordon: Yes! But you know what: Being data competent isn't just about skills. It's also about attitude.

Joana: What do you mean?

Gordon: It's about being critical about where the data has come from, if you can trust it, and whether it's been analysed properly or not. There are so many potential biases that can affect or even distort analytics, so that a *critical mindset* is really key for working effectively with analytics.

Joana: Makes sense, data is not God-given. I'll keep that in mind. But back to my original question: What role could I play in analytics in this organisation do you reckon?

Gordon: You could certainly evolve into an analytics project manager. They are key in bringing the business and data science sides together. You would have to manage not just data analysts, but also database architects first and then database administrators. There are many roles that revolve around analytics, you know. Here's a diagram that shows you some of the key roles involved in an analytics initiative (see Figure 13.1). Think about whether you would like a job as an analytics manager Joana.

Joana: A fascinating perspective, thank you Gordon. Just one last question: Where can I get support? What resources could I use to keep learning about analytics?

Gordon: Find a young data analyst to have lunch with regularly, like a reverse mentoring. Enrol in an online course on advanced analytics, like those available on Coursera or Udemy. Follow analytics instructors on LinkedIn, such as Data Science Central. Why don't you go ahead and create an informal business analytics interest group right here in our company? Sorry Joana, gotta run now.

▶

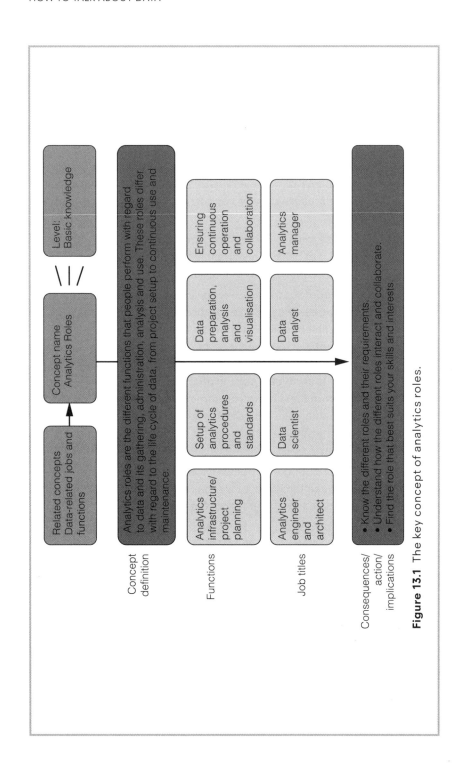

Figure 13.1 The key concept of analytics roles.

As the dialogue above illustrates, the journey to data fluency is a never-ending one. Sharpening your skills, keeping a critical attitude towards data, and connecting with others are key in this endeavour.

As Gordon indicated in the dialogue, it is also important to understand that there are different *roles* in the analytics field that have different functions with regard to data (see figure). An analytics team only consisting of data scientist would not get very far. It needs to be supported by IT architects and engineers (especially for the infrastructure planning and setup phase), database professionals and administrators, and finally the business side to make sure the data and the way that it is delivered actually provide value.

Besides mentioning the importance of a critical data attitude, the dialogue also makes reference to *resources* that can help you in your journey to data fluency. So be resourceful when it comes to learning analytics and don't just follow analytics experts on social media. Like Joana you can reach out to specialists in your own organisation, in your professional network, or among friends. You may even organise informal brown bag lunches in your department, where recent analytics trends are presented and discussed.

This book has covered the basics to understand and communicate data. Building on this, you can now delve into more advanced topics and *trends that will shape the future of analytics*, such as artificial intelligence, distributed analytics or maybe even quantum computing – a whole new IT paradigm. Monitoring these trends and translating them into business opportunities when the time is right, is an important part of data fluency. To whet your appetite, here are a few analytics topics that you should keep on your radar (Table 13.1).

You may notice that this list contains both enabling technology behind the curtains so to speak (such as quantum computing or edge analytics), as well as so-called frontend trends such as self-service analytics. To keep up to date with these trends, we recommend websites such as Gartner.com or following institutions like Data Central or outlets like Infoworld.com. Meetups are also a great way to get in contact with analytics professionals, as are LinkedIn online groups (find them at meetup.com and linkedin.com).

Next to these trends it is also important to keep up with the software *tools* used in analytics. For basic statistical analysis of data software

Table 13.1 Analytics trends and what they mean.

Analytics trend	What it means	How soon it will be relevant to organisations
Cloud analytics	This trend simply refers to the fact that more and more (especially large) data sets and (their analysis software) are hosted on servers outside of the organisation creating and using it. The analytics takes place 'in the cloud' as opposed to inside the organisation.	Already here
Cognitive computing	Algorithms to analyse unstructured data, such as documents, to assist people in complex decision making.	Very soon
Collaborative analytics	Today data is often interpreted by single data analysts who then communicate their insights to decision makers. New interfaces allow multiple people to analyse data together (remotely, or on-site) and annotate it together for better decision making.	Very soon
Distributed analytics	To run faster or reduce the infrastructure burden (and cost), analytics and data management tasks can be distributed across multiple servers and then coordinated. The same algorithms run across each of the nodes, processing a subset of the data. When the processing concludes, the data sets are aggregated, or brought back together, to generate collective insights.	Already here
Edge analytics	When data is gathered through sensors (such as temperature) and its analysis takes place in the same device, this is called edge analytics. It speeds up the time to react which is important for Internet of Things applications (think of elevator problems for example).	Already here

Analytics trend	What it means	How soon it will be relevant to organisations
Hybrid intelligence	This term refers to the vision to couple human and machine intelligence to boost decision quality – a best of both worlds approach to use human expertise and intuition in combination with artificial, data-based intelligence.	Not very soon
Mobile analytics	Simply the use of analytics software on your mobile phone which requires special interfaces and graphic displays, as well as new data storytelling formats such as scrollitelling.	Already here but not mainstream
Quantum computing	This designates a paradigm shift in how to enable faster computing that is no longer based on the two-states (0 or 1) bit, but on basic computation units (called quobits) derived from quantum mechanics that can have multiple states. This is a fundamentally new way to build a computer, but it can also be used as a new way to conceive different kinds of algorithms. It will boost our big data analytics capabilities.	Not anytime soon
Transparent AI	Currently not all recommendations by neural networks or other AI algorithms can be retraced or explained. Transparent AI, however, emphasises fully transparent machine learning where all steps of the algorithm (and the data it used) can be retraced and the criteria for decision making are reported.	Very soon
Self-service BI or self-service analytics	Self-service business intelligence or self-service analytics designate the trend to make data analysis software easier to use, so that almost everyone can conduct data analysis, regardless of their analytics skills.	Already here

packages such as IBM's SPSS or even Microsoft's Excel can do the job. Most analytics teams, however, work with programming software such as R, Python (also a programming language) or commercial (hence expensive) packages such as SAS or RapidMiner. Great and widely used tools for the analysis and visualisation of data are Tableau (now owned by Salesforce) and Microsoft's Power BI. These two are often referred to as visual analytics packages, as they emphasise the graphic presentation and exploration of data. They are often business analysts' first choice when presenting data as interactive dashboards (graphic compilations of key performance indicators).

This may now seem like a lot on your plate. Just take it step-by-step. Here is a simple, five step action plan that we recommend to ensure your data fluency stays relevant and current.

1. Talk with others about what you have learned in this book, share your learnings and ask probing questions.
2. Download trial versions of simple analytics packages (for example, at tableau.com) and play the sample files provided in that package to learn about their logic.
3. Immerse yourself in data projects and initiatives, perhaps first in a support role and act as a translator and connector.
4. Identify in which skill you still need to improve (perhaps the statistics, or the storytelling, or the bad news part) and try to improve step by step in that domain (for example, by enrolling in an evening, online, or weekend class).
5. Help bridge the IT-business divide by offering training (you understand best what you teach), presentations, or developing tools like tutorials or concise glossaries and analytics FAQs for your organisation.

Whatever the next step is that you take in your data fluency journey, we wish you much success and the best of luck. Here are your final take-aways and caveats.

Key take-aways

- Understand the organisational embedding of analytics in terms of team roles and responsibilities.
- Find a role that first allows you to speed up your learning curve and then gradually move into more central functions.

- Keep abreast of new developments in the analytics field, particularly the latest trends in artificial intelligence.
- Establish a set of useful resources for your analytics journey, including colleagues, online tutorials, or people and institutions to follow on social media.
- Become a translator among the different analytics roles and help them collaborate fruitfully.

Traps

- Never consider your data fluency journey finished. Keep on learning.
- Do respect people's job roles and understand the scope of their work.
- Don't deep dive into every analytics topic you encounter. Think about whether it fits your future profile or not.
- Do help others increase their data fluency by sharing your knowledge from this book, using simple and accessible language and illustrative examples.

Further resources

To keep your data fluency up to date, regularly check in with these premium outlets:

https://towardsdatascience.com/

www.gartner.com

www.visual-literacy.org

References

Agler, R. and De Boeck, P. (2017). On the interpretation and use of mediation: Multiple perspectives on mediation analysis. *Frontiers in Psychology, 8*, 1–11.

Bailey, K. D. (1994). *Typologies and taxonomies: An introduction to classification techniques.* Sage.

Baron, R. M. and Kenny, D. A. (1986). The moderator–mediator variable distinction in social psychological research: Conceptual, strategic, and statistical considerations. *Journal of Personality and Social Psychology, 51*, 1173–1182.

Bünzli, F. and Eppler, M. J. (2019). Strategizing for social change in nonprofit contexts: A typology of communication approaches in public communication campaigns. *Nonprofit Management and Leadership, 29*(4), 491–508.

Cho, H. and Sands, L. (2011). Gain- and loss-frame sun safety messages and psychological reactance of adolescents. *Communication Research Reports, 28*(4), 308–317.

Cramer, D. and Howitt, D. (2004). *The SAGE dictionary of statistics. A practical resource for students in the social sciences.* Sage.

Field, A. (2018). *Discovering statistics using IBM SPSS statistics* (5th edition). Sage.

Fritz, M. S. and Arthur, A. M. (2017). Moderator variables. In *Oxford research encyclopedia of psychology.* Oxford University Press.

Griffiths, D. (2008). *Head first statistics. A brain-friendly guide.* O'Reilly Media.

Jaccard, P. (1912). The distribution of the flora in the alpine zone. *New Phytologist, 11*(2), 37–50.

Miller, J. (2017). Hypothesis testing in the real world. *Educational and Psychological Measurement, 77*(4), 663–672.

Porkess, R. and Goldie, S. (2012). *Statistics.* Hodder Education.

Prochaska, J. O. and DiClemente, C. C. (1982). Transtheoretical therapy: Toward a more integrative model of change. *Psychotherapy: Theory Research & Practice, 19*(3), 276–288.

Prochaska, J. O., Redding, C. A. and Evers, K. E. (2008). The transtheoretical model and stages of change. In K. Glanz, B. K. Rimer and K. Viswanath (eds) *Health behavior and health education: Theory, research, and practice* (pp. 97–121). Jossey-Bass.

Rosenberg, B. D. and Siegel, J. T. (2018). A 50-year review of psychological reactance theory: Do not read this article. *Motivation Science*, 4(4), 281–300.

Rucker, D. D., Preacher, K. J., Tormala, Z. L. and Petty, R. E. (2011). Mediation analysis in social psychology: Current practices and new recommendations. *Social and Personality Psychology Compass*, 5(6), 359–371.

Rumsey, D. J. (2016). *Statistics for dummies* (2nd edition). Wiley.

Sivertzen, A. M., Nilsen, E. R. and Olafsen, A. H. (2013). Employer branding: Employer attractiveness and the use of social media. *Journal of Product & Brand Management*, 22(7), 473–483.

Steindl, C., Jonas, E., Sittenthaler, S., Traut-Mattausch, E. and Greenberg, J. (2015). Understanding psychological reactance: New developments and findings. *Zeitschrift Fur Psychologie/Journal of Psychology*, 223(4), 205–214.

Index